ISBN: 978-1-7353859-0-7
Printed in the United States of America

Table of Contents

Dedication

This book is dedicated to the memory of my grandmother, Edna Earle Pollard, "Mema," a fierce woman of strength and courage who was completely dedicated to serving her family and others. She loved with a deep compassion built on truth. She never gave up on anyone or anything. She was relentless in her faith and work ethic. She was resilient and a force to be reckoned with.

Acknowledgements

God, thank you for helping me to reconnect with who You intended me to be.

Will, when I look back, I see how God had a plan for us long before we ever knew. I am so grateful I get to call you my husband, my best friend, and my soulmate. There is truly no one like you. You make life fun and adventurous.

Stephanie Pollard, I am so glad that God blessed us to walk together through life as sisters. Your love is loyal, and your strength is incomparable.

Carolyn Hill (in memory), your love was unconditional, and your encouragement kept me pressing on. You were a great source of spiritual wisdom for me.

Sandy Jones (in memory), you were a connection of love and light that created so much joy in my heart. You were such a beautiful, graceful, and merciful woman.

Debbie Johnson, thank you for believing in me and praying for me to find God when I was lost.

Tolga Musa, thank you for your teachings of wisdom, knowledge, and culture. I became better equipped for life, my purpose, and loving all beings because of you.

Tanisha Stevens, thank you for your wisdom, wit, truth, and prayers. Your prayers are always so powerful and meaningful to me.

Brian Urban, thank you for always being consistent, for listening, for holding me accountable, and for showing me different perspectives.

Jennifer Whitley, thank you for saving my life and for being the greatest childhood friend anyone could ever ask for.

Nikki Williams, thank you for your positive energy, vision, and encouragement. You were the one to help me better understand myself. Thank you for taking a chance on hiring me, which opened the door for me to have a great support network, better preparing me for life.

Foreword

Girl Behind the Smile is based upon my return to what my grandmother taught me early on in life. I had wandered from that wisdom for many years. Those daily doses of wisdom she shared, which I could not understand at the time, later returned to my memory when I needed them the most.

Over time, all the situations in my life have collectively revealed my life's purpose: I was created to provide hope, to inspire, and to help others heal mentally, spiritually, emotionally, and physically. I believe that everything is connected, and everything happens for a reason. As we go through life, we experience many things—some good, some bad—but it all works for a greater good, a greater purpose. I like to think that life is like the star quilt my great-grandmother made me: it is composed of many different pieces intricately fashioned with both light and dark patches; but as a whole, it makes a beautiful star.

I debated whether or not to publish this book since it contains so many personal details of my life, but on August 8, 2019, I received confirmation, and I knew I must write this book. If my story transforms but one life in a positive way, I will have fulfilled my purpose. It is not easy to peel back your life and let others look inside. Each experience that I revisit brings old emotions back up with it. But I thought of those who may have walked in my shoes, those still trapped in prisons of their own. How could I not tell them how to be set free? My intent is not to dishonor anyone in the sharing of my journey, only to provide my personal perspective on these experiences in order to encourage others and hope they might "pay it forward."

As you read my story, may you experience love, grace, freedom, and a refreshing in your spirit.

Peace, love, and joy to you always!
Natalie P. Parrish

Part I: Caterpillar
(8-14 Yrs. Old)

Chapter 1
Beginning

As Mama was driving us to school to one day, she began crying. Between the sobs, I could hear her saying, "I don't want to live anymore." I was about eight years old, riding in the passenger seat next to her, with my sister sitting behind me in the back. I will never forget the look on my sister's face. Could she hear Mama? I was torn between the sympathy I felt for Mama and the need to protect my sister. I said what I could to comfort Mama, to let her know we loved and needed her, while also turning around to ensure my sister was okay. Although I could not see it at the time, in that moment, I was using my skills and gifts; something that could never be taught in school. While that day in the car was traumatic, and I will forever remember it, I do not resent that moment, nor Mama for it. When I look back, I can see how I rose to the occasion with strength, and through various situations like it, my skills in caring for people sharpened over time. These gifts and skills, given to me from a greater teacher, created a desire in me to help heal our world one person at a time, one animal at a time, and one situation at a time; not in the limelight, but behind the curtains of life.

My Mama—she was always beautifully dressed, with every piece of clothing perfectly paired and pressed. The reds and pinks of her lipstick and blush looked like they were pigmented from the finest of rose gardens. She was petite. Her nails were always manicured, and her skin was flawless. She loved the idea of being a mom and having a family, and in those early years, she did the best she could to be a good example for me and my sister. She stayed at home for a while and then attended school to be a registered nurse. It was her desire to be a working mom and show her daughters how important it was to get an education. During this time, she provided structure, enrolling us in dance, baton, and gymnastics. She even made us attend beauty school, because she was concerned my sister and I were becoming tomboys. For the most part, life was good, but every so many months, Mama would leave me and my sister with the babysitter or by ourselves and be gone. It never was memorable, until my late elementary school years when my parents divorced. Then, there would be times that we stayed with her when there was little to no food in the cabinet. I felt the heaviness of questioning if I was equipped to take care of my sister, but I realized there was no option, it was just necessary. We avoided telling our Daddy or grandparents about Mama. We did not want the family fighting. I later came to understand that the emotional abuse my mom had endured as a child started to show up in her adult life. She needed to escape. She also thought that buying material things would bring her happiness.

My father was a small tenant farmer. I describe him as a farmer because most farmers are one with the land. Farming was his identity. He was a strong and dedicated man committed to working the land. I remember how his hands felt as he lifted me into bed at night: dry, calloused, and sometimes blood-stained from all his hard work. I can still feel those strong hands combing my hair in the morning before school, creating the tightest ponytail that could not be undone, not even on the roughest days on the playground. Daddy worked from sun-up to sundown. I remember him being tired a lot. I understood at an early age why he was tired. The work never stopped, and the weather never allowed for a standard routine. Such is the way of life for a farmer and the farmer's family.

Individually, my father and my mother were fascinating people. Our friends and neighbors loved coming to the house when only one or the other were at home, but when they were at home together, everyone would scatter. Their arguments were the worst! It became about who could say the most harmful thing to irritate the other until the argument escalated to throwing and breaking things. This pattern unleashed a ripple effect of toxicity and hardship that troubled our family for two decades. From my perspective, Mama did not know how to genuinely love as a wife, and Daddy desperately desired the love and attention that Mama was not able to provide because of her unresolved emotional childhood trauma. This cycle showed up later in my life as well.

My sister was mostly quiet growing up. She was also gentle and shy. She played with her stuffed animals and kept to herself. For many years she did not talk much, and if she did, it was mostly to her stuffed animals or our animals on the farm. I think the most amazing thing about her was her connection with animals. They loved her! She does not recall much from the early years of our childhood, but I became good at distracting her with games, dancing, or singing when our parents were fighting. We would either turn up the radio, or I would take her into the cubby closet in my room where we would play with our stuffed animals. I remember we had Glo Worms, Pound Puppies, Care Bears, and My Little Ponies set up in cradles and play pens with blankets. We never were much into baby dolls. My sister and I were close. She would get on my nerves because she was my little sister, but I was very protective of her.

As for me, I was social for the most part, oftentimes silly, sometimes emotional and shy, depending on the situation. I've been told by many people (and this is supported by pictures) that I walked around dancing, singing, and laughing, but when the harmony was disrupted with my family or friends, I felt that disruption very deeply, spending a lot of time observing, thinking, and analyzing it all. I was always observant of everything happening around me regarding others' emotions, but who I would allow myself to be depended on who I was around. At an early age, I use to worry about my family's problems and the personal struggles of each family member, and the same was true for my friends. One of the biggest things that would bother me would be if others were excluded or bullied at school.

I thought there was something wrong with me all through my school years because I never really cared about any school subjects except writing a little. I cared about relationships. Even though I received awards for being kind and friendly, I was an average student as far as my grades were concerned. I really thought something was wrong with me. I would later discover through multiple personality profile assessments that I was born a collaborator, communicator, influencer, and encourager, one who is highly empathetic, compassionate, and intuitive. Unfortunately, there are no subjects in school that specialize in these areas. I think these people are labeled "socializers" in school. I got called that a time or two, especially in my middle school and high school years! When I discovered I was an empath later in life, my whole life started to make more sense.

Unfortunately, the ebb and flow of life at home with my parents and worrying about our family suppressed my personality at times. I was consumed with how I could solve the problems my family and friends were experiencing. I remember the heaviness of it, feeling like I was taking on others' problems myself, and I could not let them go. At night, I'd look out my bedroom window, dreaming of how I could help the world when I grew up. That dream died for a long time, but I reflect on it now, especially when I hear the songs "Paradise" and "Landslide" because they accurately paint the picture of what I felt looking out my bedroom window, dreaming.

Chapter 2
Nourishing

When I was growing up, we shuffled back and forth between Mama and Daddy's house and our paternal grandparents' home. During this time, it felt like I was living two different lives. My parents had dated when they were very young. Part of the reason they got married was to get Mama out of her abusive household. When I think about who they are as people now, it is clear to me that they were incompatible. The incompatibility was obvious in the continuous arguing, yelling, shattered possessions, and the spending sprees that followed to try to make it all right again.

My parents never displayed love towards each other. They constantly argued, and they avoided one another, purposefully never being home at the same time. Witnessing all of this created abandonment and trust issues for my sister and me. The sadness of the situation led to emotional eating, and I was extremely overweight at a young age. Because of this, I encountered some bullying in elementary school. I remember being called names, sometimes even in jest. I would outwardly laugh most of the time, but the truth is, it hurt on the inside. The only time I would stand my ground was if others were being bullied.

I am thankful I had my grandparents when I was growing up. I knew I was fortunate at the time, but in looking back now, I often sit in awe of how lucky I was to have them in my life. They showed unconditional love and stability for our family. My grandmother was the backbone of our family, and I now realize how she was the best gift of my childhood. Her gifts of love, wisdom, and spirit-filled living continue to pour into me, even though she has since passed.

Chapter 3
Growing

Edna Earle, my grandmother, my Mema, was the person I most identified with in my family. Because we were raised in a traditional southern family, and I was the oldest girl, I spent most of my time on the farm with my grandmother. We would start each day by saying our prayers and making the beds. Our family would eat breakfast together, and then work in the fields. Mema and I would come in at lunch to prepare meals for everyone. I used to get so annoyed about setting the table. She would make me do place settings with plates, napkins, forks, knives, and spoons and then test me on it, even if we used paper plates on Taco Saturdays! I said, "Why do I have to do this every time? I am never going to need to do this." Mema would then say, "It is important that you have good manners so you can help others when you go visit them. You should always be helpful wherever you go. One day you are going to go to college and make something of yourself, and I want to make sure you are prepared. We may not have much, but there ain't no excuse for not having good manners."

Our meals served not only my family, but also extended family who lived on the farm and others in the community who helped on the farm. During a time when racism was still prevalent in eastern North Carolina in the rural farm communities, I remember asking my grandmother, "Why don't other families ask the Black and Hispanic people to come inside and eat at the same table?" Even though I was child, I could see the discord in her eyes, as I knew there was more to it than she wanted to say. She said, "Baby, always remember, you treat everyone the same. God loves everyone." I would start with more questions, but she said, "One day, you'll understand. Just remember what I said." When I think back now, although we battled unintentional and intentional racism in our family and extended family, my Mema, who was raised during the Great Depression, was a progressive for her time and place. She was the person who influenced me strongly to be an advocate for all people. When she spoke her mind amongst our family, everyone listened. In a traditional farming family that was uncommon, but the respect people had for her was immense and incomparable. She could do every task on the farm and do it faster and better than anyone else. No one could outwork her or outlast her. For the men in the family, this went a long way. So, if she asked for something or said something, everyone listened, and everyone supported.

After we would all eat together for lunch, we would go back into the fields to help, or we would clean up the barnyard. During the evening, we would prepare dinner. In the summers, the evenings consisted of sitting on the porch during sunset swinging, sometimes shelling peas or snapping beans. It was hard work, but it taught me so many life skills. During this time with my Mema, she would teach me things to help me in life. All these things centered around themes of peace, patience, kindness, love, understanding, self-control, faith, and hope. One of her favorite sayings was, "Baby, pretty is as pretty does, and it's what in here (she would point to her heart) that matters, do you understand what I am saying?" My first response was, "But Mema, you are pretty on the outside and the inside." She said, "Thank you, but we are not supposed to focus on those things, because pride and ego can get in the way of what really matters." Then she would say, "Do you understand?" I would smile and say, "Yes." Then she would say, "Yes, what?" I would say, "Yes, Ma'am." I then asked, "Why do I have to say, 'Ma'am'?" She would say, "Because it is a sign of respect for your elders."

My favorite times with Mema were the experiences that I would now call spiritual. I can hear her singing and humming any time I reflect on my time with her. Her favorite hymns were "Amazing Grace," "Because He Lives," "In the Garden," and "Blessed Assurance." One time, Mema gave me this card with my name on it that she had saved in her old wind-up jewelry box. It said: "Natalie, 'Christmas Child' Joshua 1:9 'Have I not commanded you? Be strong and

19

courageous. Do not be frightened and do not be dismayed, for the Lord your God is with you wherever you go.'" I said, "Mema, what does all that mean?" She said, "Baby, the Lord delights in you like Christmas. Jesus was born on Christmas, so if you are a Christmas Child, it means you are special. It also means that the Lord is always going to watch over you and protect you in your life." I believed everything she told me because she was the person I most connected with and identified with in my family.

My other favorite times with Mema were spent in flower and vegetable gardening. I remember all the butterflies that would fly around when she was working in the dirt. I would get caught up in the moment, imitating the butterflies and trying to get them to land on my hand. I still know that feeling now, when time slows down, and you know this is a moment you are going to remember forever. I would watch the butterfly's wings flutter in slow motion, taking in all of its vibrant, intricately patterned colors, wishing and wanting to be like it; wanting to fly with freedom and grace. I would watch as the butterflies descended, as if to connect, as if they were stopping in to say hello. I asked Mema why it happened. She said, "Baby, it's about the spirit you carry within you. They sense it. It's the same with all God's creatures." In the garden, in the dew of the morning, when my sister and I got tired of working with my Mema, she would let us lay in the cool, black dirt. Our pillows were the bellies of stray dogs Mema had taken in, who we claimed as our best friends. It was not unusual to overhear me and my sister whispering to our dogs, "I love you because you ani-, mals don't hurt like people do." Fast forward to my adult life in difficult times. It would not be unusual to see me curled up next my dog, who brought me a type of comfort that is incomparable. I treasured my times with my Mema and the compassion she taught me for all beings, human and animals.

Troy was my grandfather, my Papa. He was nothing but guts and grit. He smelled of Marlboros and his skin was tough as leather from his days of farming. He was a no-nonsense person when it came to working, but had everyone belly-laughing when it was time to play. He spoke the truth, even if people did not like it. He was known for saying, "Don't ask unless you really want to know." To me, the coolest story is about when my grandfather was diagnosed with cancer. I am told that Mema and her prayer partners prayed for him to be healed. During that time, Mama became pregnant with me. When my Papa returned to the doctor, there was no cancer. I think he was healed by the prayers of those women. I also believe God answered those prayers, because He knew I would need my Papa in my life. From my Papa, I learned: "Be good to your word; stand up for those who can't stand up for themselves; and tell the truth, even when it is hard."

Even though there were tough times in our household growing up because my parents were not compatible, our farm and our community was full of people who came together to help, work, teach, and to celebrate one another. It was because of that environment that I learned so many life survival skills grounded in integrity, perseverance, and compassion. We worked the land, harvested, cooked, and enjoyed meals together, not just within the family, but as a community. We learned how to care for animals, visit the sick, and chip in to help each other when there was loss in the community. The work was hard, but the reward was great.

Part II: Metamorphosis
(15-24 Yrs. Old)

Chapter 4
Entering the Cocoon

Life came closing in abruptly. On October 16, my Mema told me she had cancer. I was fifteen years old, and I still remember the evening well. The harvest moon hung in the night sky, glowing brightly through the darkness. I ran through the field and landed, head hanging down, on our pasture fence, trying to catch my breath. The thought of living without Mema had never crossed my mind. All I could think was the person that loved me, the person that understood me, and the person who allowed me to feel free as a child was going to be taken from me. At that point, I asked God, "Why would you do this to us?! She is our rock. She is the backbone of this family. It will all fall apart without her." This is when the innocence and purity I felt in chasing the sun and running free with my animals on the farm was stolen. The light in my heart started fading until it became dim and eventually went dark. In there, I cocooned myself.

The trips back and forth to the hospital were hard on the whole family. They had to drive into the "city," and they were not used to driving in traffic. Both my Mema and Papa were still productive and efficient workers on the farm, so when they were gone on these days, Daddy felt the loss of their help, trying to keep everything going. The hospital bills started to pile up, and it was more than our family could handle. I began to understand what my Mema had always told me, "You are going to get a college education, and when you get out there working, remember, don't ever ask anyone to do anything you ain't willing to do. You hear me? You be fair, and you will do well." Watching my family become financially stressed during that time, I decided that I really wanted to understand how finances worked and how to be good at managing them, so I could come back and help our family.

During the periods my Mema took chemo treatments, I continued to visit each week. She amazed me with her strength and hopeful outlook. I recall the time she and I raked the driveway after her chemo treatment. It was hot and humid in the dead of summer. She had long sleeves, long pants, a light scarf, and a hat on. I was so tired and ready to quit, but I could not bring myself to as I watched her work and persevere through the heat and sickness.

The more time I spent with my Mema, the more it created jealousy with Mama. I know it was so important for Mama to be a good mother, and she was in a lot of ways, but occasionally the emotional trauma that she never dealt with would rear its ugly head. The sicker my Mema got, and the more time I was with her, the more animosity it created with Mama. She loved my Mema, too, but she wanted me to love her more. She did not understand the mentality that it takes a village, and that you do not love one family member more than the other, you just love them differently. My Mema, because of the person she was, never spoke ill of my Mama. My Mema would always say, "Baby, remember, your Mama loves you, it's just in her own way, but she really does love you. Remember that long after I am gone, and try to understand what it has been like for her."

My childhood years went by, and we were living in between multiple houses. After the divorce, both my parents had remarried and my sister and I went back and forth between both houses every other week, per court orders. I got so tired of it. I would always ride with Mama in the front seat where I'd then be dropped off at Daddy's, or we'd pick up my stepdad's son. In most of the pick-ups and drop-offs, I had to keep my stepdad's ex-wife and my stepmom from fighting my Mama, because Mama would make passive aggressive comments to fuel the fires that were still blazing. I often felt caught in-between all of this, always trying hard not to let my feelings show, hiding behind a smile that said, "I'm ok. It's all ok. It will all be alright," when I knew inside it really wasn't.

Chapter 5
Enclosed in the Dark

The news of my Mema having cancer was too much, too fast, and I was becoming a teenager. I do not remember what self-destructive habit came first. I found myself in a push/pull relationship with myself and others. I was a complete roller coaster of emotions. I was in high school, and I started partying. Before long, the up all night and sleep all day lifestyle, along with dwelling on the fact that my grandmother, my favorite person, was going to die, left me in a state of depression. Life seemed too hard. I thought, *My God, if I already feel this tired of life by age sixteen, I do not think I am going to make it in life.* Then a day came when I woke up, and I did not feel like dealing with it all anymore. I just wanted to permanently sleep and rest. I downed a whole bottle of pills from Mama's medicine cabinet.

That day, my friend called me and asked me to go to

the pool with her. I decided to go, like it was just another regular day. I was emotionless and hopeless on the inside, but smiling and projecting that everything was okay on the outside. While I was swimming in the pool, thinking about everything in life, I lost my hearing and my sight. My friend asked me what was wrong, and I remember trying to get the words out, but that is all. I woke up in a hospital bed looking out the window. I overheard the doctor and nurses saying, "Her heart rate is still too high; she should not get up." The only other thing I remember during my stay is that my Mema came in and gave me this angel bear with golden wings. She handed it to me and said, "When you press its heart, it says, 'You are my guardian angel. You are my special friend.'" I still have that bear to this day. Mema said, "It's all going to be okay. God takes care of us all. Remember Joshua 1:9 and how He named you and calls you Christmas Child." When she told me that, even though I was depressed, she carried so much light within her, there was no space for darkness when she was with me. I underwent evaluation and was in the hospital a few days, then I was discharged.

I am so thankful that my friend came and got me that day to go to the pool. She saved my life, and I will be forever grateful to her. Will, who was my best guy friend at the time, was also instrumental in supporting me. Rather, we supported each other, because he had a lot going on in his life also. During this time, he told me that he had heard my Mama had tried to take her own life when she was sixteen years old. This piece of information actually helped open my eyes. I had just begun to wonder about Mama's childhood, wanting to understand more about what she went through, in hopes it could help me and my sister to face any life traumas that might come our way and to manage the stress of things differently. I saw how she suffered. I wanted better for her and for us.

Soon after my discharge, my mom and stepdad recommended I attend church camp with my friends. Although I was caught up inside myself during this point in time in my life, I look back and see how hard my stepdad tried to provide stability and consistency in our home during this time. He fixed me breakfast every morning and helped me with the laundry. I never knew if others knew what happened with my overdose. When you live in a small town, families try to keep these things quiet because when one person knows, everyone knows. Honestly, we never really talked about it in our family.

In addition to church camp, another therapy (which became an important part of my whole journey) was spending time with my animals and listening to music. "Melissa" and "Into the Mystic" were my songs that made me feel free at the time. During those years, I was fortunate enough attend concerts and see artists such as The Rolling Stones, The Allman Brothers Band, Lenny Kravitz, The Doobie Brothers, and Jimmy Buffett, and I went to many festivals where various other bands performed. I also enjoyed many motorcycle rides, which was a freedom unparalleled. There is just something about feeling the wind on your face and the warmth of sunshine on a long open road. Despite the controversy of hanging with a motorcycle club off and on during my teen-age years and working part-time as a parts girl at a motor-cycle shop, I learned a lot during that time that helped me to understand life better. I was a bit naïve, so the exposure helped ground me in knowing in how to deal with the real-ities of the world. I explored a variety of identities including grunge life, romantic poet, free-spirited hippie, and biker girl, and I learned so much through the process. The biggest lesson I learned was that no matter the person or group, at the core, everyone just wants to feel like they belong, that they are loved and validated. I am just thankful I made it through and did not get into any trouble; well, except that one underage drinking ticket at one of The Allman Brothers Band concerts!

My grandmother's condition worsened. To watch her be sick broke the hearts of everyone in our family. Things started to go downhill financially, and then Hurricane Fran struck our farm, setting into motion a decline from which neither our family nor our farm ever fully recovered. From the day my grandmother was diagnosed with cancer, it seemed like our farm was slowly dying along with her. It was like there was a desperate sigh of sadness from the land and the creatures she cared for. I continued to help Daddy at the farmer's market, and would do so even after starting at college. I think one of the toughest situations to endure as a farming family is doing the best you can, even if the year doesn't produce the crop you expected. You still have to try to sell what you have because there is nothing else, and the family depends on it. I remember times when I would try to sell vegetables that didn't look as perfect as they should. We'd be hurting at the end of the day because we'd make only forty dollars, which wasn't even enough to pay for the boxes, gas, and labor it took to get the vegetables to the market. Because of those experiences, I am extremely passionate about supporting our small farmers, because farming is hard work and farmers often go unrewarded and unrecognized. Whether it is a natural disaster or a tough year due to the weather, these few, hard-working people have to feed the entire world!

Between the ages of seventeen and twenty-three were probably the toughest years of my life. It all started with an event that I carry with me even to this day. At seventeen, I became pregnant. It was the summer before I went to college. I was partying all the time. My lifestyle was so crazy, and I was so scared. I knew I couldn't have a baby. I wasn't healthy enough to take care of a baby. In our small town, I knew there'd be talk, and I did not want to shame my family. At that time, I could not bring myself to even imagine telling my family. I think that was partly because we had enough to deal with, and I did not want to add to the stress level. I did not want to have an abortion. Neither did I want to have the baby and give it up for adoption. I remembered what Mama had been through, being adopted, and all I could think about was the emotional trauma she went through with the family that had adopted her. North Carolina did not allow underage abortions at that time, so I had to go to South Carolina.

It was the worst day. My friends were driving my car, and I remember crying while everyone was doing drugs, but this was the life I was living at the time. We got to the place, and it was in a pretty bad area of town. I was just five, maybe six weeks along, and they questioned whether or not they should perform the procedure. They indicated there may be difficulties because I was not far enough along, but I decided to proceed anyway. I did not know until I heard other stories that it was not normal to be awake and aware and without any sedation whatsoever while it was happening. I felt every bit of the horrible mental, physical, and emotional pain that came with it. I have to stop here and say that I would not recommend abortion today, but I also would not pass judgement on a woman's choice to have one. I can tell you from experience that there is no need to shame or tear down a person who has had an abortion because they feel those emotions without the added judgement of others upon them. I can also say that during that time, I was not in a place spiritually to fully understand the repercussions of this choice, which I would carry for the rest of my life.

My recovery was a struggle. I stayed at a friend's mother's house, and she cared for me over the weekend. I had to pretend like I was out of town with friends so my parents would not find out. During that time, all my friends decided to go to a party. They did not want to leave me, so I went along and sat on the tailgate of the truck while everyone was socializing and partying. When it was time to go, because so many people were intoxicated on the substance of their choice, there were very few people sober enough to drive. After the girls and guys paired up for the night, I was asked if I could ride in the back of the truck on the way home. I never was one to put anyone out, even with my condition at the time, so I got into the back of the truck. I remember this so vividly—too vividly. I had to lay down because the pain I felt was so bad. Suddenly, I started bleeding. I had blood all over myself. All I could do was cry. I remember crying and thinking to myself, "This is what I deserve for what I did."

If I could speak to that girl back then from where I am now, I would tell her, "You didn't deserve that. That is shame and guilt trying to ruin your life. When you do not know better, you cannot do better, as I learned later in reading Maya Angelou's books. When you are imprisoned, you do not make the best choices. God is not a God of condemnation. He only brings conviction, so you can do better, live better. He is a God of limitless compassion and forgiveness.

On Monday, and because it was summer, my sister and I had to go to work with Daddy to harvest the fields. That day still stands out to me. I was hurting and still bleeding. It was July. It was ninety-seven degrees outside, and there was brutally high humidity. It was hazy, and there were very few breezes, if any, to cool you off. I stopped to catch my breath and leaned over and grabbed my stomach. Blood started running down my leg. I thought I was going to pass out. I heard Daddy coming, and all I could do was wipe off my leg with spit and sand because I was so scared he would see it. Daddy started calling to us, "Keep it moving, girls, we got a lot of work to do." Uncharacteristically, my sister popped up and said to Daddy, "You leave her alone, she doesn't feel good." "What in the world has got into you?" he said to her. "Don't you talk back to me like that." Then Daddy looked at me and said, "What's wrong with you?" I said, "I don't feel good." He said, "Go, sit down in the truck." I was sick; not just sick with pain, but sick in what I had done. I know everyone says you have a choice, and I know that, but during that point in my life I did not feel like I had a choice, and I was imprisoned in so many ways. I was drowning, but I kept trying to come up for air. Eventually, I began to heal physically, but emotionally, the wound remained.

Shortly after that tragic moment in my life, I started dating a guy that took care of me and my sister. He was good to me and my family. Though I thought it was true love at the time, I later realized it was an extremely toxic relationship. With all my insecurities and abandonment issues coupled with his anger when he was drinking, we began a seven-year downward spiral both together as a couple and as individuals. My intent here is not to shame or blame anyone, but rather to use the following stories to help others to be aware of or even to prevent someone from staying in a toxic relationship like this. I only hold a space of love and forgiveness for this person, and I wish him well because I saw how he really battled with himself, like I battled with myself. It is important for me to share some things that happened during our relationship, because they were situations that made me stronger. They also served a purpose later by giving me the perspective I needed to help others who have been in similar situations.

The first time we split up, he left messages. He was upset, asking me to come back. I was living away at college part of the time, and the rest of the time I lived with him. The relationship was so unhealthy, and one night when we were at a party, I left. All my things were still at the house, including my dog. When I did not return his phone calls after some time, he threatened to harm my dog and said no one would be able protect me. I started worrying, caught in the mindset that no one would be able to help me, and I was especially worried about my dog. I felt like I had to go back for my dog, but also, I was trying to hide what was happening because I thought I could not be helped. When I returned, my dog was not there. He told me he would never kill an animal. He said he was just mad. He promised me he had just given the dog away, and a friend even verified his story. "I want to go see her," I told him, but he said he gave her to some stranger outside of a store, and there was no way to find him or the dog. I became hysterical. I started crying, and I could not stop. I felt responsible for whatever happened to my dog. This is one of the problems with these kind of relationships. Shame, guilt, manipulation, and control get disguised as "love" and it turns into an unhealthy attachment that warps the mind.

The second time I tried to leave, he had been out drinking with a neighbor and came home drunk. We started arguing off and on while he was watching TV. I was up and down, doing laundry and cleaning. I think cleaning was a coping mechanism for me, thinking I was cleaning up (fixing) the situation. He went into the back bedroom, and I walked back to see what he was doing. For the first time, I believed demon possession could be real. He had a gun in his hand, and he raised it to my forehead and started speaking in a language I did not recognize. When I looked in his eyes, it did not even look like him. In that moment, I had tears streaming down my face, and I said, "God, if you help me right now, I will turn my life around." He passed out and fell backwards. I was in shock. I could not believe it! I had had a second close call with death, and I survived. I called his mom to let her know what was going on, and I left after that. I started to change and really believe I was on a different path—but then I went back to him again! My grandmother had become extremely sick, and they moved her to hospice within her home. I suppose that may have been the reason I went back. It would have been too much loss in my mind at the time, and I was so broken already. I just wanted the pain I felt in my heart to stop.

My grandmother's health was declining. The thought of being without her hit me so hard that I quit my college job because I wanted to help take care of her. After all, she had taken care of me and shown me consistent, unconditional love. The last week was the roughest. I never left her side for

38

a week. She would come in and out of consciousness, describing things she saw and still trying to pray. She tried to let each person know what they meant to her and to speak words of wisdom she wanted to leave with them. I remember on one of those last days, she seemed to be asleep, because her eyes were closed, but she was mumbling that Jesus was going uphill to a field full of grass to lay down a blanket. He told her not to be worried, that He was preparing a place for her to be with Him. She grabbed my hand and said, "I pray for you and your sister to always have discernment, to know the difference between right and wrong and do what is right." I am thankful for that last week I had with her, but I was so devastated by all this that I had not slept, and I was reaching delirium from all the emotions. My family finally talked me into going home after seven straight days of not leaving her side. That night I went home to pack clothes, shower, and try to get some sleep. As I was sleeping, I was dreaming that Mema was telling me goodbye when suddenly my eyes opened abruptly, and I gasped for breath with an outpouring of tears. I thought, *I need to go back to my Mema.* That's when the phone rang, and it was Daddy telling me Mema had just passed. At this point in my life, I still had a lot of questions about God and spirituality/religion, but one thing was certain, I know that my dream felt real. It was my first loss, and it was the most difficult loss of my life.

I was struggling, and my emotions were on high. I was still in this toxic relationship. My anger had always started to rise when we would argue, but now I started fighting back, which made everything worse. I did not feel like myself. The grief of losing my grandmother coupled with our relationship troubles let loose a fire that nearly burned us both to ashes. In a heated argument one night, I started yelling because he was in another drunken stupor, and I could not take it anymore. He was laughing as he took his palm and smashed my glasses into my face. Not long after that we went out with some friends, and once again he had too much to drink. Our friends were staying in the spare bedroom. I remember lying on the hallway floor as he had taken a coat hanger, wrapped it around my throat, and started choking me. I looked up and saw our friends peeping through the door, but they did not step in to help. The last thing I remembered was waking up on the floor where I had apparently passed out. I managed to get up. Looking in the mirror, I swallowed my salty tears and whispered to myself, "Your Mema would not want you living like this. She wanted you to make something of yourself. Remember Joshua 1:9 ... "

This was the third and final time I left the guy. All the years of toxicity flashed before my eyes as I thought about my dog, the gun to my head, the smashed glasses on my face, being strangled with a coat hanger, and being left at home in the country during a snow storm with no power or heat because he stopped and decided to drink at a bar and instead of driving home from out of town. I wanted more in life, and I wanted out of this toxic relationship. I knew I was done, only it does not end so easily when you are in a co-dependent relationship. I told him I was leaving. He said the worst thing and the best thing he could have ever said to me: "How do you feel knowing your Mema is looking down from heaven thinking you're such a whore?" While I know this was not the right response, I finally had no fear in that moment. I started screaming at him and jumped on him. We wrestled through the house. I paid for it in the end, but one thing was for sure—I was done.

I thought it would be easy after all that, but leaving was only half the battle. The next few months began a toxic cycle of me calling him and him calling me. It was a roller coaster of emotions. I was living the co-dependent relationship I had seen as a child with my parents, and the same was true for him. As I took a step back, I knew we did not belong together, and he agreed. We went our separate ways. That is when the healing began.

I share this story because there are usually patterns to these types of relationships, and awareness is key. I think the most telling sign was that we truly brought out the worst in each other. I believe that is because hurt people, hurt people. I now understand that every person is worthy of living a life of love, grace, and freedom. If you are in a toxic relationship right now, I pray for the cycle to be broken, for the chains of imprisonment to be broken, for healing to begin, and for you to live your best life.

As if the struggle of a long-term, toxic relationship wasn't enough to deal with, within the same year, our family lost their farm and my great-grandmother and great-uncle who lived on the farm with us. And all this in just a few years after my grandmother's passing. Daddy had to start over, and it nearly killed him mentally, emotionally, spiritually, and physically. He was even forced to ask my ex for work. I never faulted Daddy for it because I knew no one was going to hire him. All of his hard work, years of experience, and passion for farming wasn't something that easily translated to a resume. He had to learn a whole new trade in his fifties in order to make a living. He didn't give up, although he drifted off into his own world during this time, dealing with the pain in unhealthy ways. For months, my sister and I spent our weekends looking for him just to make sure he was still alive. To say it was a hard time would be an understatement. I was working full-time and trying to heal from my toxic relationship. My sister and I would drive around at night, stopping and looking in different places for my dad. I remember calling my friend Will, to tell him where we were in case something went wrong.

Chapter 6

Transition

As I was trying to adapt to living by myself for the first time, I was ready to establish true independence, not "needing" someone to make me feel whole or "needing" someone to make the time go by. Guess what happens when you escape everything and are ready to start fresh? *You* are still there alone with all your baggage! In the midst of sitting and reflecting, I turned into a zombie when I started to process everything that had happened to me: the recent deaths of my great-grandmother and great-uncle, our the loss of the farm, the stress of looking for Daddy at night while I worked full time during the day. My stepmom at the time said, "I really think you should see a doctor and get on some medication to help you through this, even if only for the short term." Up until that point, I had believed that it was important to work through your troubles in order to heal properly. But this time I needed help, and I knew it. I started seeing a doctor and taking an antidepressant.

Thank God that during this time I had a friend at work who really helped me through my issues. She kept saying that she was praying for me to find God, for me to experience His love and see His goodness. I would just smile, but honestly, I was in a hopeless place. One night, as I lay in the dark on my bedroom floor listening to "She Talks to Angels" on repeat, I thought about everything that had happened in my life. I thought about my Mema's wise sayings and what she had taught me about God. I remembered how she had lived her life and what she represented. I pulled one of the many Bibles I had been given as a child out of my nightstand. I laid my hand on it, crying, and said in a frustrated tone, "God, if you are real, I really need to hear from you! I really need you to speak to me! My Mema taught me about you, and I could see she had a relationship with you, but I need for you to make yourself real to me because I can't go on living like this." I continued, "I am going to randomly open this Bible—please speak to me!" I opened my Bible, and it fell open to Psalm 27. I felt what can only be described as a supernatural force of warmth, made of a thousand waves of love and vibrations of peace. I have never felt anything like it before. I just knew I wanted more of it.

While I had never before seen the importance of church and religion, over time, I decided to go to church for community and support in healing. I no longer had my Mema, and there was nowhere else to go because my family was falling apart at this same time. The really good thing about attending church during that time was that my stepmom was instrumental in getting my Daddy to attend church with me. What a double blessing it was when Daddy also felt the presence of the Holy Spirit and started to get his life back on track. During that time, a family friend prayed over me and again, I felt the presence of God on me. I decided to get baptized and so did Daddy. I was so excited, I decided to invite my friend Will. I think one of the most beautiful things about Will was that he was there at those key moments of my life: at the funeral when my grandmother passed, helping me move during those college years, and during my baptism, which was such a significant event. My baptism was memorable, to say the least. Not only did I feel the most peace I have ever felt in my life, when I came up out of the pool of water, I created a wave big enough to soak the pastor. To this day, he still tells the story about how he wore waders in the baptism pool, but the wave I created coming up out of the water was so big, it soaked his clothes inside his waders. I am sure it was because I let go of a lot of baggage that day!

Part III: Butterfly Revealed
(25-37 Yrs. Old)

Chapter 7
Emergence

Something happened when I came up out of the water during my baptism at age twenty-four. Things changed quickly in my life. I thought I was in a position where I could come off the antidepressant, so I did. I did not know, however, that I was supposed to come off of it slowly, under a doctor's supervision. For two weeks, I felt like I was in a constant state of emotional adjustment. I would not advise coming off of an antidepressant this way, but I persevered through, all the while reading books about healing and restoration. After two weeks, I felt like the person I was supposed to be; the person I had lost so long before. I was coming out of the dark back into the light. I was emerging from my cocoon.

That one big wave in that baptism pool created a ripple effect in my life. I began to focus on helping people find their way and encouraging them through their life struggles. My testimony was not like others I had heard, nor did it follow tradition. I did not find God in a church, nor did I find him in religious studies or conversation. The presence of the Holy Spirit had greeted me as I sat on my bedroom floor, broken. I had asked God to make Himself real to me, and He did. Prior to that time, after my grandmother was diagnosed with cancer, I had been uncertain of what I believed. For so many years, I had read books about different philosophies and religions, as I went seeking to find the truth for myself. Sometimes I felt nothing, but at other times I felt a darkness that did not align with my inner spirit. This is what I call a warning sign or a red flag. Listen to it! It is there for a reason. My belief is based on pure experience. It is not influenced by any religion, by any man-made beliefs, or by other people's opinions. Who wants to be told what to believe? We get to choose what we believe, and I want others to find the joy, peace, and love that I have found. Finding God, for me, did not mean *no more* life challenges; it meant that life challenges became more bearable and doable with God in my life.

Life was better with God, but I longed for a relationship like I'd had with my Mema. I prayed about it, and when I got lonely, I resorted to a mantra I came to recite often: "God is my everything, He understands me, and that's all I need." I can see now how that prayer was a product of the pain and loss I had already experienced up to that point in life; it was the result of not wanting to trust and love again.

As I started to grow in my spiritual life, my relationship with one of my grandmother's best friends, Mrs. Carolyn, started to grow. She called me periodically and checked on me. Like my Mema, she often had sayings filled with great spiritual inspiration and life wisdom. She would send me cards, bookmarks, and gifts that were nothing short of a beacon of light when I needed it the most. She made me believe in myself and was always so encouraging. This is one of those times I thank God for my unanswered prayers. I like to think, now, that even though I prayed that God was enough, He gave me the gift of Mrs. Carolyn as an angel here on Earth.

Chapter 8
Preparing for Flight

A s I began to find the joy in life, so did my best guy friend, Will. There are not enough words to describe the big personality of Will, but I will give it a try. He is multi-dimensional. Unique would be an understatement. He is funny, loving, and magnetic. He is vibrant on some days, and on other days he is cool, calm, and patient, just enjoying his solitude. He is often funny in a way that is borderline inappropriate, but he walks the line so finely, it's as if he knows just how far to go. When it is time to work, he is driven; a warrior out to triumph the task. He thrives on competition. Outside of work, he's known for grand gestures that far exceed what you expected or which you may never have expected at all. He has a great talent for being surprising and shocking. His romantic grand gestures are few, but when they happen, they cannot be matched by any man. He loves in a way that makes me feel free. This is the very reason why we always stayed connected. He knew exactly how to love and support me.

Will and I were progressing down the same path of wanting to have a better life. We were both abandoning former, destructive routines and building a future. We thought we were just friends, not seeing what everyone else was seeing. We started hanging out all the time, because we were aiming to be positive and trying to leave all the negativity behind. During those days, that meant spending less time with *some* people. I want to emphasize, here, that I have loved all my friends and family, but there comes a time when a season ends, and a new one begins, and there are times when you have to create healthy boundaries and even distance. After a while, people asked if we were dating. We'd say no, and we really believed it! Then a close friend, who had previously pointed out that we would be married one day, said, "You're hanging out every day, and you enjoy each other's company. Why don't you just call it what it is?" A year after dating, we got engaged. Three months later, we got married. It happened so fast that everyone was convinced I was pregnant, but I was not! This time is best described by the songs, "Is This Love?" which was our song, and a song Will liked to sing to me called "Crazy Love." Boy, does Will have a great voice! It melts me every time. While we both loved each other, we were scared to get married because of our family histories of destructive relationships and divorce. It was just so important to us to get it right the first time. While saying our vows, I was crying with joy, but also sweating from anxiety, and so was he! He wiped the sweat from his forehead with a handkerchief and then wiped the tears from underneath my eyes with the sweaty handkerchief. We both laughed, and you could hear the laughs echo throughout the church.

When Will and I got married, I was fortunate enough to gain another female figure in my life. Not only did God deepen my relationship with Mrs. Carolyn, but He also sent me Sandy. Sandy was one of Will's best friend's mothers. He spent a lot of time with their family over many years. She was like a second mom to Will and would become the same for me. These two women were great mentors to me and filled a void that I needed when I lost my grandmother. I needed someone to talk to who could understand me. It was hard being highly intuitive, empathetic, and compassionate. During that time, I did not know how to get outside of myself and use my gifts more wisely as a strength.

In the first year of our marriage, our baggage from our previous relationships crept in. I had so much worry and anxiety on the inside, all centered around shame, low self-esteem, and abandonment issues. This, coupled with my husband's tendency to walk away or leave in order to deal with an issue, made for a complete disaster. I needed affirmation that he loved me and wouldn't leave, but that was the opposite of how he'd learned to respond in dealing with arguments. This went on for a year! Finally, he said, "You can take a chance and enjoy life with me, or you can spend your time worrying about what could go wrong, believing I will leave. I will do my best to try to communicate better, instead of walking away." Honestly, that is the best thing he could have said to me, because it really made me press in to try to control my verbal response based on my unhealthy thought patterns. He also agreed to work at better communicating his feelings *verbally*. In looking back, both of us were struggling with being vulnerable. When you spend most of your time in fight or flight mode, over time, vulnerability becomes more difficult. I think we had just spent too much of our time in fight or flight mode. While we made that agreement with each other, stuck to it, and prayed about it, other challenges flooded our marriage from the outside during the first seven years.

In our first year together, my father-in-law came to live with us. It started innocently, when I asked him to come for a visit. During this time, I prepared the first sit-down meal Will and his dad had ever had. Although I had known Will and his family when I was in high school, I did not know the depth of their struggles. I would babysit Will's sister sometimes, while his mom was working, and Will was out looking for his dad. As my father-in-law's visit turned into a four-year stay, I learned about his time in Vietnam, Post Traumatic Stress Disorder (PTSD), bipolar disorder, and his struggle with alcoholism. At the time, I wanted to be a good wife and help restore the relationship between Will and his father. By providing a healthy daily routine, we did help Will's dad get sober. He had only two lapses in over a decade! While good things came about from that living arrangement, we learned over time that it was not healthy for any of us, and it was highly stressful. We had different people in and out of the house who we were also trying to help then, and it was creating co-dependent relationships instead of healthy, independent lives. At times, it even put us in danger.

While this was going on, I was also working full time and working on my MBA. Will had just left his place of employment to start a new business. On my salary alone, we were considered below poverty level. We told ourselves we could do it because I was the daughter of a farmer, and he was the son of a builder. Growing up, we had both learned the meaning of feast or famine. But despite our optimism, the situation brought about a lot of stress, and I would later find out that Will was dabbling in drugs again to cope with the slow growth of his new business. We made a lot of mistakes when we first started the business. Although that is the best way to learn, Will took it to heart, seeing himself as a failure. After a long winter where it took everything I had to get him out of that recliner, I knew the substance abuse had started again.

To compound the problem, there were new problems in my family. My parents were both on their second marriages and struggling with various issues, and my Papa was facing some major life changes. When my Mema had passed away, my Papa and I had become even closer. I think it was because I went to see him almost every day for six months after she passed. We would just hold hands and cry. My Papa was not a man who cried often. The only time I ever saw him cry other than over the loss of Mema was when Will proposed to me (he was present for the occasion). My Papa was sick off and on, and we had to move him into low-income housing. This was a hard transition for us all, but as time went on, my Papa quickly discovered the joy of being one of only a few men in an apartment building full of women. His stories during this time kept me laughing on most days. I would get calls from him about the dinners and dance parties he'd get invited to. Many times, when I'd go to visit and clean, I'd find that his apartment had already been cleaned, and there were lots of casserole dishes in the fridge. I would say, "Papa, you told me you needed your house cleaned and some more meals." He would say, "I just wanted to see you, Bean Blossom." Leave it to a farmer to give you an endearing name like that. He was something else!

My Papa struggled with Chronic Obstructive Pulmonary Disease (COPD) for years. The last two years of his life, he was in and out of the hospital. Twice, before he passed, he was rushed to the hospital, and I was with him. I was fortunate enough to ride with him and the rescue squad and talk to him on the way. Of course, I was worried, but he was making jokes, as he often would, to lighten the mood. The last time he was in the hospital, Will and I were with him before he lost consciousness. His last request was a bacon, lettuce, and tomato (BLT) sandwich, so I walked to the hospital café to get him one. When I got back, I sat by his bedside while he ate his sandwich and watched TV. He said, "You know, Little Bit (another one of his endearing names for me), if I can't smoke, watch TV, or even enjoy a meal anymore from being sick, then that ain't living. I need you to be okay when my time comes. I have had a good life, you know." I said, "I know, it's just so hard." Not long after he finished his sandwich, he lost consciousness. That was on a Friday right after work. I remember the doctor said he would not wake up after that, it was just a matter of making him comfortable. He passed on a Tuesday with his family surrounding him in prayer. The most memorable moment for me came on the Sunday before his passing. I was with him and had just finished reading his favorite book in the Bible, the book of John. I was just so sad, not knowing what to do, so I began reading aloud from his Bible. I sat in peace when family and friends started to come in to visit. I reached over to tell him I loved him and squeezed his hand (which I would periodically do), and in one struggling breath, he opened his eyes in a quick flash and said, "Love you." I will never ever forget it because the doctors had said he would not regain consciousness. This was another time that confirmed to me that there is so much we do not know, and that with God, anything is possible. I considered that moment as a gift from God and a representation of His love, which I much needed.

My Papa passing away was not the only loss Will and I experienced in a short time. Within a two-year period, Will lost both of his grandmothers and an aunt. I felt honored to be with many of Will's aunts when they said goodbye to his paternal grandmother. It was hard, but I felt good, giving my best to provide comfort to everyone since I had already experienced so much loss. On top of this, Will's cousin was in the hospital with cancer. For two years, we spent most of our time visiting the nursing home and hospitals and grieving. It was a hard time for everyone.

In 2009, once we emerged from the grief, we were excited to finish up our dream house, making it what we thought would be our final home. We had fun decorating and landscaping. This home was everything we ever wanted, or so we thought.

Not long after we settled in, a new set of challenges presented themselves. My mother divorced from her second husband. After attempting to live with her family in Georgia to start over, her emotional issues from her childhood re-surfaced, along with anger towards life and God. We ended up having to move her back here near us because it was too much for her extended family to deal with. This set into motion what would become the greatest identity crisis of my life. What I could not see at the time was that I was allowing my mother's anger towards me with her words (which had nothing to do with me) define me as a person. It took me six years to figure out how to best manage the situation. I had to learn to understand that she lashed out at others that she blamed for her unhappiness because she had not taken time to heal from her issues. Since she no longer had a husband to blame, I was her target. I began to see the war within her and how she was conflicted. She would *say* how much she loved me and my sister, yet her actions communicated something different. I honestly believe she loves us and has always loved us; it is just that her emotional trauma is so deep, and she has not yet dealt with it. I think this is because of the stigma associated with mental health and her desire to cover up that anything was "wrong." For now, my Mama continues to struggle and remains imprisoned in her mind. For this reason, I make a point of talking to my family and friends about the hard things in life. Because of my life experiences, I understand the meaning of the sayings, "truth equals freedom" and "the truth will set you free." Everyone's oppression is different, and the focus of my life and my prayers is to help oppressed people find freedom, no matter what the oppression is.

Chapter 9
Finding the Right Flowers

In 2012, things started to take flight. That fall, Will and I attended a marriage retreat. This was a life-changing experience for us both, especially Will, because he experienced the presence of the Holy Spirit. I prayed for seven years before I saw this prayer come to fruition. My prayer was that he, too, would experience the power of the peace and love of the Holy Spirit. I did not want him to settle for going through the steps of manmade religion by just, "making a decision." I wanted him to believe big, as I did, and God delivered. While it was a moving experience, it was comical at the same time. It was a Sunday, and after the last message of the retreat, they played a song. Will stood up and started crying and shaking. Let me add here that before this moment, I had only seen my husband cry twice: once when his maternal grandmother passed and once when I was laying at the side of my grandfather's bed as he was dying. I had to ask, "Are you okay? You look like you are going to pass out." He said, "What is happening to me? I have never felt this good before." I said, "The only explanation I can give you is that it is the presence of the Holy Spirit." My response was not based on what someone told me or what I read. I just remember feeling exactly as he described when I was laying on my bedroom floor in my twenties. When the Holy Spirit wraps you in His love and peace, you cannot fight the emotions, no matter how hard you try.

The same month of Will's experience, I started a new job at a biotechnology company. At the time, I had no idea this would be a pivotal period in my life. This is where my life started to take flight. I was like those butterflies from my Mema's garden; as things changed around me, I began to feel my wings start to move freely. Even though it was a challenging time, it was an exciting time. I had finally found the right flowers, and I flew from one to another, rising to the potential that others had said I had, but that I could never see in myself before. During this time, the song "I Still Haven't Found What I'm Looking For" resonated with me. I was pleasantly surprised and shocked as these new people in my life helped me see that God had bigger plans for me. Up until this time, I had always limited myself, and they made me see that I was capable of so much more!

It all began with the manager who hired me and the co-workers that supported me. I know, now, that the whole set-up was a blessing from God. My manager helped me

64

understand myself through a series of personality profile assessments. It was a "wow" moment for me as I read the assessments. It was scarily spot-on, as if the person who wrote it had been riding around in my back pocket my whole life! Hundreds of experiences began replaying in my mind, and for the first time, I saw them within the context of *why* I had struggled to find my way growing up! The dream I had so long ago, staring out my bedroom window as a little girl, wanting to change the world, was because I was an influencer, collaborator, communicator—all relationship-based strengths. When I was little, I never had an answer for what I wanted to be when I grew up. In that moment I understood why: growing up in a small town with limited opportunity, my strengths could not have been encouraged into a concrete career that I wanted to pursue.

For the first time ever, I had someone with the same personality type as me who was helping me understand myself: an Extrovert, Intuitive, Feeling, and Perceiving (ENFP) person, which are the charismatics, enthusiasts, and creatives of the world. My manager was brilliant, and I was so ecstatic to have her in my life. It was great we could relate to one another, and it would be easy for her to understand how to advise me. I am thankful she had the foresight to realize that I also needed a mentor with the opposite of my personality profile to help me grow and see different perspectives. The first person she asked was not available due to a transition and increase in responsibilities. I know now, in looking back, that everything happens for a reason, because the person I asked and accepted really helped me in the areas of self-awareness and life wisdom.

It was all sunshine and rainbows with my manager who was like me, of course! Finally, a match that understood me! She was warm, fun, and exciting. She also had a thirst for knowledge, for learning, and for sharing what she learned. We could brainstorm the grandest of visions and make a hundred connections, like fireworks on the 4th of July. It was the first time I met someone whose conversations and thought process were the same as mine. I did not have to adapt my way of being and communicate it in a structured way in order for someone else to understand it. We both talked to think, asked a million questions, answered them all in the same session, and then were completely energized in the end, whereas we tended to leave most people exhausted.

Everyone needs a person like my first manager. She is my person I go to when I need to re-energize and refuel. She is that person who has always cheered me on. She encourages me, challenges me, and pulls me out of a pity party, if I start to lean that way. She has a zest for life and reminds me that I was made the same way. She was the first person to help me see all the connections of my life. She showed me how my exhaustive quest to find the right career needed to be viewed through a different lens. She explained how I was made to give hope and inspire and how, while I had been searching for the right career, I had been living my purpose all along, wherever I went. She even gave me examples of what she had seen. She had observed that when others were struggling, I helped uplift their spirits. She had also noted that I tried to help people live a better a life. She saw that I had an ability to zone in on the issues of others with my intuition and get them to open up. When they felt better because they had someone that they could talk to, the healing would begin. That is when I discovered that I was so focused on the future that I was missing the impact and joy of the present.

Then life with my new mentor (opposite in style of manager) was different, but it was also good for me. I believe the overall good from this learning experience will far exceed what we know in the here and now. I liken it to the end our lives when we meet God, and He shows us our life. It is in those moments that He shows you the positive impact you had on others that you did not get to see during your time on Earth. I have already had the privilege of mentoring others and passing on what I learned as a result of this mentorship.

It was a tale of every emotion a person could experience. My mentor brought me into the truth of myself, my strengths and my weaknesses. When we reviewed the "good" stuff, it was so much fun! He made me realize I was resilient and resourceful due to my life experiences. When we got to the "bad" stuff, I initially had a hard time listening. I said I was listening, but I was hearing, not listening. I learned the difference in that mentorship! In looking back, I can even recall some conversations and how my incessant talking was a form of trying to escape the reality of what he was saying.

He was very patient with me, but also intentional in his responses to me, to help me understand how to better control my emotions. It was from him that I learned how to catch myself, slow down, and be thoughtful about my words and actions. I also learned that sometimes the best response is no response. People who throw stones often live in glass houses, and the assumptions that we make come from the stories we tell ourselves and not always from the truth. I had a life-defining moment during this time, only I did not know it was life-defining when it occurred. After all the challenging times in my life, my mentor reminded me of the story of Joseph, only I did not know the story of Joseph then, so he had to tell it to me. In summary, he said, "It is important that you keep doing good by everyone regardless of their response. Just keep pressing on, being you, and trusting God is working everything for a greater good." I didn't know then either how important those words were in the moment or how they would show up again and be the basis of what prompted me to write this book.

Probably the most beautiful thing I experienced in this mentorship was learning that the world is bigger and more diverse than I had experienced growing up. Through the relationship with my mentor and him being from a multi-cultural background, it was the first time in my life I began to openly love and see everyone for who they are, without awkwardness, and to embrace the differences. Being raised in the rural southern part of the United States, my experience with diversity had been somewhat limited, so when

I entered college and the workforce, I really struggled. I felt self-conscious about every word I spoke to someone who was "not like me." The environment in which I had grown up had created this unintentional barrier between myself and other people which officially collapsed as a result of this mentorship. I came to realize that when you are genuinely acting from a place of love, love floods the gates of fear until they come crashing down. I now understand that fear-based thinking was a false perception that created a false barrier, which kept me from doing what we are all called to do—just love one another genuinely.

As if one mentor opposite in personality was not enough in my life, my mentor at the time introduced me to someone else within his team that he thought would be good at coaching me. This guy was the definition of accountability and consistency. He was very skilled at taking my emotional responses to situations and asking questions that helped me arrive at the answers myself. By the end of our conversations, I would be calmer, be thinking more clearly, and I would have a solution for my issue. He taught me how to take strategies and organize them into actions. In fact, my method and logic became so refined over time that people began to see me as a data person rather than a creative. Who would have thought it could ever be true! The truth is, I just became balanced, which was what I very much needed. Through my roller coaster of personal and professional challenges, he always reminded me to be consistent and be accountable. After multiple times of stating that I wished I could work for him, that wish came true.

In my time with his company, I am grateful to have had these mentors and many co-workers and executive management leaders who supported me. There were interactions that I had there that I will forever remember. I remember this strong woman whom I deeply connected with, and after getting to know her, we discovered we had similar backgrounds in rural eastern North Carolina, with our grandmothers being huge influences in our lives. One day, after an inspection, as I was walking off, I heard her say to the others standing around, "That girl right there is special. One day she is going to be a star." While it was not my desire to be a star, I needed to hear that encouragement to keep pressing on. As I continued walking to my car, tears came, and I said, "God, thank you for sending people along my way to help fill the void from losing my Mema's encouragement." If you have ever battled with low self-esteem, shame, or great loss, you will know what I mean when I say that she replenished the water in the well of my soul, possibly without even knowing it.

It was during this time that I became very sick. Prior to 2013, I struggled with sinus infections and was on antibiotics up to four times a year for over fifteen years. In 2013, I became very tired, but this was a different kind of tired. I became so fatigued by that summer, I could not walk a flight of stairs without getting out of breath. This was not me. I had lost all my energy. After going to many doctors and specialists, they found nothing, only saying, "All your results are normal. You are in perfect health." Then the battle of the mind started. Something in me said, "Keep pushing for the answer. This is not a normal feeling for you." Finally, I visited an ENT and insisted on a CT Scan. I was not going to take no for an answer, and I think that is the place you have to be to see change happen. The CT Scan revealed a "mass" covering my entire right sphenoid sinus cavity. I was then sent for an MRI to gather more information on the probability of whether it was a tumor or a fungal ball.

After the doctor said the word "tumor" as a possibility, the conversation was a blur. I remember getting in my car and just sitting there with all the "what ifs" starting to swirl in my head. Then I stopped and went into soldier mode, thinking, "What do we need to do and let's get it done." After receiving the MRI results, the doctor was certain it was a fungal ball. It had to be removed, and it had to be removed soon, because they discovered the bone that creates the barrier to the brain tissue was slowly being eaten away from the infection. The infection was so bad that the doctor said if it hadn't been dealt with in one or two more months, the fungus would have eaten through the bone into the brain tissue. Because of the severity of the infection, I was put on a heavy antibiotic leading up to the surgery. I did not respond well to the antibiotic. I lost mobility and flexibility in my right foot, which made it hard to walk. They did not know if this would be temporary or long-term. I ended up coming off the antibiotic right before the surgery because it was also affecting me

71

emotionally. The surgery was scheduled, and in addition to removing the fungal ball, it included the reconstruction and widening of the space in my sinus cavity so everyday debris could easily move in and out to improve my allergic sinusitis issues. There were many risks because the sinus cavity was located behind my right eye. But through much prayer, I came through with no complications.

At the same time all this was happening, I felt this overwhelming conviction to attend an international missions and culture course and learn about different cultures. Once my mentorship had allowed me to break through the false barrier of being worried about how to communicate with people from different cultures, it was like I went off the deep end in wanting to love everyone across the world. I started the course and ended up pursuing a certification, which took four years. I remember the first in-person class experience. I was the only one attending who was not a pastor's wife and who didn't have the same well-thought-out plan as everyone else there. When I was asked what had brought me there, I simply answered, "I think I am supposed to be here; maybe because God wants me here. I am not sure, but I just follow my intuition on these things."

Throughout 2014 and 2015, I was feeling rather good, and my check-ups were all clear. Not only was I completing my international missions and culture certification, but I had this desire to read about vitamins, herbs, and essential oils. I considered this my decompression time; my distraction from the world. What was I going to do with that knowledge? I was not really sure then, other than using the knowledge to help make myself healthier and then share what I'd learned with others.

In the beginning of 2016, I got the call to go visit Mrs. Carolyn because she did not have much longer to live. I am so glad I had time to say goodbye to her. She had been my substitute grandmother since my Mema had passed. She had been a woman of great spiritual wisdom to me. She was a rock. It was also during this time that Sandy, the lady who was like a second mom to me, was diagnosed with cancer. It was a rough start to the year. I began to feel sad and tired. I thought it was all from losing a particularly important role model in my life and then having to watch another one battle for her life, but that was not the root cause.

The sickness had returned! Once again, I was extremely fatigued. I could not climb a flight of stairs without struggling to breathe. I started taking naps in the evening because I could not make it another step after work. This was not your usual, "I had a long day at work" tired. I could not make it until bedtime without collapsing on the couch. In fact, I became so dizzy and tired, I left during an inspection at work, which I normally would have never done. I made an appointment with another ENT, who came highly recommended by another doctor I trusted. The dreaded news came. The ENT doctor ran a scope and told me that I had another fungal ball, and I would need surgery to have it removed. While the ENT doctor complimented the work of the other ENT surgeon, he noted that the opening would need to be just a little wider in order for any everyday debris to exchange in and out. I was like, "Are you for real right now?! I must do this again with all the risks involved?" Through many prayers, I had another successful surgery with no complications. God bless that doctor and all the questions I asked him during that time, trying to gain surety of the situation. The possible conclusion for this happening twice was that I had just stressed myself out over time, not had the best living conditions, and the overuse of antibiotics had just weakened my immune system.

During this time, I was reporting to a manager I had always wanted to work for. He and the team I was working with were incredibly supportive of me during my sickness, surgery, and recovery. It was then that I became closer to a person who became a big piece of my life's puzzle. She became my strong spiritual partner. She was witty, poised, and soft-spoken, yet not timid in any way. When she had something to say, it was something of real substance and often piercing (in a good way) and life-changing. I admired this the most about her. I started to call her the Truth-Bringer! At times, when she spoke, I felt that God was speaking through her to me, and it was exactly what I needed in that moment. Once, when I was torn about attending a retreat, I had explained to her how I felt like I should go, but I wanted to back out. I was concerned because I knew this retreat involved a mixed group of religious beliefs and I did not want to get mixed up in anything dark again like in my teenage years. Was God calling me there for a reason? I had my doubts. She looked at me and explained the story of Moses: how he was raised, what he did, the people he was surrounded with, and how God had used him. This was a significant moment for me, and I decided to go.

Another change was on the horizon. My spiritual experience and relationship with God deepened to a whole new level I never thought possible. What started with what I thought was isolation and a heart full of tragedies still not healed, became a two-year walk with God bringing me more healing and personal growth.

Part IV: Adult Butterfly
(38-40 Yrs. Old)

Chapter 10
Fluttering

At the retreat in February, 2017, I received my first set of clear visions from God. At that time, God also showed me the pain inside a girl I would end up praying with for healing. After it was over, she was in awe of the peace that she felt. She asked me what I had done, so I explained my experience and my prayer for her. She said she had been in torment for nearly two years. I had no idea what else to tell her other than what I had experienced, which was how Jesus showed me how He saw her, what pain she was feeling, and the prayer I felt led to pray. I cannot even accurately put into words the feelings that Jesus showed me He had for this girl. It was such a deep love. It was also during that retreat that the people who had much different beliefs than I did acknowledged what had happened and indicated my connection to the "Divine" and how there would be more of that in my future. As my teacher looked at me, she became teary-eyed and just kept repeating about my connection to the divine and how I would reach people far and wide.

As the music began to play, we went into a meditation time. I drifted into a state I cannot accurately describe. I am not sure if I was awake or asleep, but I will forever remember the clear, vibrant pictures I saw flash by, with different scenes and people. At first, I was swimming in the ocean effortlessly, then it changed to me sitting on the shore with Jesus, all dressed in white. My husband, Will, appeared beside me. Then I saw a friend sitting with Jesus. The vision moved on, as if I were walking to different lands with Jesus holding my hand and showing me different things happening in the world: wars, and places where people needed help. I also saw a child crouched down on a dirt road in the distance, looking at me. I walked to greet the child as if it were waiting for me. The scene switched, and then God showed me a family I knew, and how the chains of anxiety would be broken for the father/husband. The family was standing together, smiling, as a picture of the father and husband's lifelong struggle played out and culminated in triumph.

In the summer of 2017, not long after the visions, I felt compelled to go on a mission trip to Cuba. I wanted to go to experience the world. I wanted to love people and share in their experiences. I wanted to offer them words of comfort and pray for the sick. I wanted more of what I had experienced at the retreat in February of 2017. Not only did I want to do this mission trip, but I also wanted to take a leisure trip to Paris with Will for our anniversary at the end of the year. I had just emerged from being sick and was grateful. I had these awesome visions. I was ready to start living and start doing everything I had dreamed of doing. Why not? What was holding me back? I had been holding myself back, but not anymore.

I started preparing for Cuba. All I could think about was Cuba. In fact, I am fairly sure everyone around me was tired of hearing me talk about Cuba. I was asked to help with the kids at vacation Bible school when we got there, and I started to panic. I could not explain it. I cried to myself and thought of a million excuses as to why I needed to serve on a different team. Then, in a time of reflection, I discovered that my desire to avoid the assignment was related to me trying to minimize my interactions with kids. Being around kids reminded me of the abortion I had when I was younger. What made this so real for me is that through the years, I had dreamt of what my child might look like. I wonder if the dream stemmed from a longing for the natural mother/child bond or if the dream was a gift from God, showing me that my child was okay. Either way, my child had a face, and the picture always stayed with me. As I thought of every possible excuse as to why I could not serve the children, the trip leader kept encouraging me by saying, "It is going to be fine." He did not know my backstory, but I trusted him because he had proven himself time and time again both in the workplace and at church.

We set out on our trip to Cuba. It was surreal as we entered through security at the Santa Clara airport. There were military police everywhere. Everything was serious, and the first thing I thought was, *Oh God, this is not the place for my jokester husband.* We made it through. Will made it through! As we started interacting with the people, my eyes were opened in so many ways. Experiencing an impoverished area is quite different than seeing it in the media. How quickly my thought process flipped! I saw the lack here, but realized there was lack in the United States, too, just in a different way. Not only that, but I saw with my own eyes something I had been skeptical about my whole life: spiritual warfare. I had always heard that God's words are living words and still relevant, yesterday, today, and forever, yet I never understood what that meant until our time in Cuba. If there was ever a picture of astonishment, it would have been a picture of my face during our walks around the countryside each day. We encountered people overcome with evil, lost to the extent of demonic possession. We saw people plagued with skin diseases and agitated by flies from the lack of water in their community. What struck a deep and unparalleled chord in my heart was the love within the families and communities to care for the sick and how the believers celebrated and praised with the most beautiful music and voices. There is just something different about worship when the people gathered are clothed in humility, which obviously comes from persevering through hardships. In our times walking in the countryside, there were a few experiences that impressed upon my memory forever, such as the following.

I remember this woman whose sister had requested that we visit her. The woman would not speak, but motioned for us to come in and sit down. I will never forget the look in her eyes. It was the first time I could feel the heaviness and realness of spiritual warfare in a room. She looked so lost and hurt, so hollowed-eyed. I saw in her eyes a mirrored reflection of myself from times past, reaching out and hoping someone would grasp my hand to pull me out of the mire, but feeling too imprisoned by the dark. We sat down, and our group leader began talking to her. She did not respond. She just sat and stared. She stared at me with those lost eyes that said, "You cannot help me." I could not stand the feeling of what her face showed, and my heart ached for her. In an overspill of emotion, I started to share my story, listening to my intuition, as my Mema had taught me. As I spoke of the dark places I had walked, and the hurt I had endured and overcome, tears started streaming down her face. Something I said resonated with her and created a response, even if only with tears. We asked if we could pray for her, and she agreed. She never talked while we were there, and I would never know what happened, but I do know that when we walked in, her hollow eyes had come to life and given way to tears, which told me there would still be hope long after we were gone.

The second most memorable experience I had was seeing dogs so malnourished that I could count their ribs, and they were overrun by swarms of flies. It crushed me. I could not let the picture of those poor dogs go. I had diet restrictions, and I had brought my own snacks, so each morning when we got our breakfast sandwiches, I would save mine in my backpack and feed the dogs on our daily walks. It was not a long-term solution, but "every act of kindness makes a difference," as my Mema used to say.

The most healing memory of the trip was when I sat under an avocado tree, and the kids started to gather around me. They kept scooting in closer, smiling, touching my hair, my face, and my arms. Although there was a slight language barrier, it did not prevent the conversation. Love and the Spirit occupied the space. We smiled, laughed, and giggled in the sunshine under the tree that day, also accompanied by a dog. Yes, it was one of the dogs I had fed along the way.

We had said our goodbyes and were well on our way back home when we had a minor issue. I was the first to board the plane with our translator, but before we stepped on board, the military police questioned our translator, and it sounded like something was terribly wrong. I could tell by the passion in their words that it looked like I was not going to be allowed on the plane. Before my translator could tell me that it was because my ticket had been torn in the wrong place, my mind raced with images of me already in a jail cell, Will having to fly home to get money, and then him not being allowed to come back into the country to get me. The mind can take such an interesting journey in just a short period of time. It just goes to show that you cannot accurately judge conversations in different languages and cultures based

on your own. We boarded the flight safely, and from that
point forward we were blessed, just barely making our flights
back home and getting through each gate just in time!

Then came the culture shock of returning home. I
never thought a short-term trip would create the culture
shock that it did. It started when we entered through the
Miami airport with everyone pushing and shoving through
the lines. I felt like I was in slow motion watching it occur,
thinking *how sad.* In the days ahead, I stared into my closet
and began ripping clothes off the hangers to bag and take
to the nearest donation center. Returning to work was the
biggest shocker, as I listened to people debate over what
seemed to be the most trivial things in the grand scheme of
life. All I could think of when people were talking was this:
while we are sitting here living lavishly and arguing, there are
people suffering greatly who show more gratitude than we
do. Then one of my mentors quickly reminded me that I was
one of those people living lavishly, too—another reason why
everyone needs a mentor or someone they can go to for a
self-check.

When I returned from Cuba, I thought I was in the
clear! I had made it through assisting with the children's
activities on the trip. Then I was asked to speak at church
about my experience in Cuba. God had pressed upon my
heart and spirit so clearly that I was to share my testimony. I
felt Him say to me: "Here is where I work things in your life
for the greater good. Your testimony will help others, even

if you do not get to see it." I replied, "God are you serious? There is *no* way I can stand on stage in front of hundreds of people and talk about my abortion, my avoidance of wanting to help kids on the Cuba trip, and how it then became a healing experience." God would not let up in my spirit. I knew I had to do it for those who were quietly suffering and punishing themselves. I knew I had to help them, despite the ridicule and judgment I might have to face. He said, "This is how you pay it forward. This is how you provide hope. You reach out with one hand to help someone, and you let go of the baggage with the other hand. Then that next person does the same thing." With my fear of speaking in front of large groups, along with the difficulty of sharing my most personal pain, I cannot believe I actually stood up in the light on stage and shared part of my story and the healing that I experienced on the Cuba trip.

As I watched the replay of my testimony, I could see that it was shaky and very emotional. I looked at it and thought, *I could have controlled my emotions better,* but I have learned that perfect is not what people are looking for. People respond to genuine emotions, not rehearsed ones. I remember, after I finished, seeing people backstage and those who were in the front rows. There were not a lot of dry eyes. As is always the case when speaking on any controversial topic, not every response is praising, supportive, and loving. As I finished up, I was told that someone wanted to speak with me in the hallway. I walked down, excited for the conversation, and a poised lady greeted me. She introduced herself and smiled politely. She said, "It is very brave of you to share your story in front of all of these people. I am assuming you had an abortion, although you did not say those words exactly. If you want God to forgive you for your sin and ensure you receive the proper healing, I can help you." I felt anger for a moment, then I realized that when it comes to controversial topics, people usually think they are doing the right thing. I paused and said, "Thank you for your offer. Yes, I had an abortion. I understand you are trying to help, but I do not think it is necessary to go through someone else to get God's forgiveness. I am healing in my own way with the help of God. For me, and those who made the same choice as me, this does not help, it only feels condemning. I realize you are probably just trying to be nice and helpful." She gave me her card and then told me to call her if I changed my mind. I know she meant well, but we all have the same access to God.

It had been a great summer. I was so excited about preparing for a trip to Paris in late fall, when I received a call from my sister. I could barely understand her as she choked back the tears. Her boyfriend had been rushed to the hospital and was non-responsive after collapsing at the gym. She was screaming over and over and all she could say was, "Pray for him! Pray for him, Natalie." As I hung up the phone, I prayed, but I did not have a good feeling. When I arrived at the hospital, my sister just kept repeating, "He didn't make it. He didn't make it, Natalie." She asked if Will and I could walk back with her to view his body one last time. As we stood over his bed, she just kept saying the same things over and over to him, "It's not supposed to be this way." This was the longest relationship she had been in, and in the days preceding his death, they had discussed getting engaged to be married. As I watched my sister, I saw her as a child again, helpless, only this time, there was nothing I could do to make it better. I felt paralyzed with a physical ache in my heart. There was nothing I could say or do. What would I say or do? No distractions like holding, singing, or dancing would make this kind of hurt go away.

There was a lot of reflection in my family during this time of loss. My sister's boyfriend was Black. It had taken years for our family to accept an inter-racial relationship, and Will and I had stood with them both. Through the tears and heartbreak my sister endured in her relationship, I saw firsthand the anguish and hurt racism causes. I got to know my sister's boyfriend. My sister would say, "You both have the most compassionate hearts for people." Any subconscious walls inside of me that had been created by environment and my upbringing had been broken by my mentor and dear friend and through knowing my sister's boyfriend. I remember I had announced at Thanksgiving and Christmas one year, "If any of you are not okay with my sister and her boyfriend, please do not come to my house, and if you show up and intentionally mistreat or unintentionally insult them, I will ask you to leave." Some people wanted to know if I was feeling okay. Everyone showed up except one person. I am happy to say that person was later transformed by the love of a bi-racial child adopted into his extended family. I have come to realize that racism originates out of fear (which is taught) and ignorance. In all my experiences, once love of another person of a different race overtakes the heart, there is no room for racism. That is because hate cannot exist where love exists, and it only takes one person to make a difference. My sister's boyfriend made our family challenge their perceptions. This further permeated the hearts of our family when we all sat together at his funeral in a Black church, grieving the loss of a good-hearted human being. There were people of all colors and cultures that showed up that day with testimonies and a message that moved the whole church. It was the first time I had been to a funeral service where multiple people got saved. Although I had never seen that offered or happen at a funeral, I felt the spirit move in that church that day. God was in that place.

The days ahead left me perplexed and without solutions to help my sister. I showed up, but I was not as strong as I had always been. It paralyzed me to see the mental state my sister was experiencing. I was struggling and trying not to show it. Maybe it was the collective pain we had experienced together in our lifetimes that just made this the tipping point. Thank goodness for her roommate at the time. She took over, and I trusted her. It was the first time I had ever trusted anyone when it came to caring for my sister.

Will and I decided to continue with our trip to Paris. We had tried for two years to take our anniversary trip, but work and personal things kept coming up, and I would put those first. Also, we thought it would be a much-needed break, because for those weeks after the tragedy with my sister's boyfriend, I did not sleep much. I was mentally, physically, and emotionally stressed. I had not told anyone, but in between the time of coming back from Cuba and the death of my sister's boyfriend, I had not felt my best. I was ready for a break.

Paris was the first time I had been to Europe. I know it sounds cliché, but I fell in love with Paris. It was even better than I imagined. Perfumes and cologne scents were everywhere, lingering like my favorite song on repeat. The smells were so mesmerizing, it left my mind in a much needed imaginary dream fog. Fashion was captivating with pea coats and peasant blouses at the turn of every corner. I thought, *French is truly the language of love.* Men would open doors, and women would laugh with love in their smiles. Both the sidewalk and museum art was so intricate in detail, that it filled my heart with emotion that I was helpless to resist. My favorite experience was encountering a beggar at Notre Dame cathedral and seeing compassion in her eyes while a musician was playing "Free Fallin" in the street. I also spoke to a homeless lady living on the street with her dog. It did not matter that we could not speak each other's language very well. The body language and the hug and smile said enough. I remember God speaking to my spirit saying, "Let them see Me through you," which led me to initiate the interaction. I also just kept seeing the love of Jesus when I would look at each of these women. I am so glad I stopped to clutch their hand, give them a gift, and then embrace them in love. I will never forget their eyes or their smiles when I showed them love. Sometimes, we just walk by those situations and either avoid them or second guess what we are hearing from our intuition or from God.

When we returned home from Paris, I noticed a change in the texture of my hair. I often looked pale, but I now felt extremely tired. I was not as upbeat as usual, and once again, I did not feel like myself. I was getting up each morning trying to motivate myself by listening to "Sound of Sunshine" over and over. I went for all my check-ups and found a flood of things I had to deal with all at once. I had low iron, parasites, 11 moles that had to be removed, chronic reactivation of the virus that caused mono, and 1 polyp in my colon. In short, I had major gut and immune system issues! After having overused antibiotics for fifteen-plus years, I opted for a different treatment. This time, I tried eating whole food, Vitamin C IV cocktails, and supplements. I worked with a doctor who was a licensed medical doctor but also believed in using holistic methods to rebuild my immune system. I had learned a lot about health and nutrition over time, and this was the most success I had encountered so far on my health journey.

At the end of that year, we moved to a new house so that we could be closer to the city, and I felt a longing in my spirit to find another church. After visiting numerous places, we thought we had made up our minds. Then one snowy day, we arrived at the church we thought we were going to choose, only to find it was closed. We then went back to one of the churches we had visited previously that day, and I knew we were in the right place. I felt that satisfying presence of the Holy Spirit that I had longed to continue experiencing. Once your thirst is quenched by the works of the Holy Spirit, nothing else will do. During that service, I knew in my spirit that this church was the next step I needed to grow my spiritual gifts and find out more about my purpose. It was another case of "knowingness" in my spirit, but without the details. I thought I knew a little bit about spiritual gifts because they often tie into other different skills tests you can get in the workplace, but I learned I really did not know as much as I thought I knew until I attended this church. Another confirmation that we were supposed to be at this church was that I had attended a women's conference there in January, just three months earlier. That conference had been a missing piece to something I was trying to figure out. I kept having this recurring dream about going up an escalator, and it was eating away at me as to why I kept having this dream. Then all of a sudden, out of the speaker's mouth at that conference came a metaphor about riding an escalator and how at some point you have to step off and keep moving with what you know until you hear differently from God. Because of these experiences, I was fairly sure this was our new church, and Will agreed.

Church was going great, and Will and I felt like we were finding and confirming more about our life path and purpose. Then our life was shaken up by a lawsuit against a company my husband owned with another person. As soon as we read the papers, I knew it was the work of evil. The action was for work that occurred while we had been on our mission trip to Cuba. The superintendent left in charge had made an error. The errors were corrected with help from an engineering firm, but it cost us dearly. I do not mean the money aspect of it, although that was a strain, also. During this time, we learned that in an effort to win for their clients, lawyers can take accusations to the extreme and stretch the truth so far that an innocent person could be sent to prison so easily. This almost happened to my husband and his partner. All I could think about was how we had been on a mission trip in Cuba trying to do good in the world, while back at home, lawyers were dredging up the youthful mistakes of my husband and our dear friend from childhood and using them to assassinate their characters, even though both of them had completely turned their lives around. I remember pausing and thinking about how many people are imprisoned every day for things they did not do. In that moment, I understood what that meant and what that felt like. The lawsuit went on for over a year, and the stress it put on both our families cannot even be put into words.

I am so thankful we found a church a month before the lawsuit started, because I don't think we would have been equipped to deal with the false accusations and character assassinations on Will and his partner without the support of our church and the prayer intercessors. During this struggle, someone told Will he would begin an intimate, two-year walk with the Holy Spirit, and that is exactly what happened. Not only did the presence of the Holy Spirit become more real to him, but Will focused in on the paperwork, diligently preparing for the lawsuit. Reviewing documentation had never been his favorite thing to do, as he preferred to work and fix things with his hands. It really ended up being a second blessing that his business savvy increased during that time. I tell people now that though the lawsuit brought a long period of stress and hurt, it caused my husband's reliance and trust in God to deepen, so to me, it was worth it.

Chapter 11
Flying

To get through the stress of the day-to-day with the lawsuit hanging over our heads, and so that we were able to keep working, we started taking classes and researching and reading more to grow in faith, wisdom, and knowledge. I found another class over the summer that had me curious. An engineer was teaching a spirit-filled living class. This seemed like an oxymoron to me, so of course, I had to go see about it! The engineer's wife had been healed from an illness and was able to walk again. He could not believe it was a miracle or healing, so he went on this journey, going through the Bible, trying to disprove healing only to come out a believer and someone who now healed other people! I must be honest: I was curious, but I questioned it at the same time. During the class, he asked if anyone wanted to receive the baptism of the Holy Spirit, which was explained to me as receiving your own personal prayer language—your spirit convenes with the Holy Spirit and your human self and thoughts do not get in the way. I think of it this way, you can use your own personal prayer language (in the spirit, the pure part of us made in the image of God) to pray without interference from the skewed thinking of the ego. I was skeptical, but I was open to seeing what would happen. The instructions were, "Just open your mouth like you are going to make a sound, and let the words flow." It did not work! I came back and told the teacher, and he said, "I get it. I am an engineer, and I was skeptical. You're overthinking it. Try listening to music to take your mind off of it, and try to let any sounds roll off your tongue." I tried it, and something started happening. It was by far the strangest thing, but it felt like the part of me that was having trouble expressing myself was resolved by this new thing called prayer language. The more I started to do it, the faster it got, and it sounded nothing like my English. I realized, then, that when I've felt there is something more out there, or something I can't explain or understand, we all feel the same way, but we all can be connected by the pure part of spirit, which is one with God. I immediately wanted everyone in the world who has experienced so much hurt and pain to have access to that feeling I had.

July of 2018 was a special month. We decided to take a last-minute extended weekend vacation to get away and clear our heads. We visited Denver, Colorado to see the Tedeschi Trucks Band at Red Rocks Amphitheater and to see the Rocky Mountains. The sight and sound of Red Rocks at sunset, with the city as the backdrop, was a memorable moment.

Reaching the top of the Rocky Mountains while listening to "Rocky Mountain High," seeing elk and the beauty of nature around us in the cool, crisp air was an amazing experience. Will and I were just breathing it all in and savoring the moments. By seeing God's wonders of nature, I felt like I was really living. I loved to travel. I loved getting out. I loved that I abandoned my fear somewhere along the way to venture out into the unknown. I really believe that I started to be able to let go as I deepened my trust in God and because I was surrounded by mentors at work. Combined, these things made me believe that anything was achievable.

A couple of weeks later, it was time for the Chris Robinson Brotherhood show. I had wanted to meet Chris Robinson since "She Talks to Angels" became a life-changing song of mine when I left the past behind and entered into a new life when I was 24. Each year, I wrote down my goals, and up until this point, I had met most, if not all, of them. I thought that if I wrote down "meet Chris Robinson" for 2018, maybe it would happen. Why not? There was nothing to lose. Will and I ended up meeting him and the rest of the band. We took pictures with the band and even got a picture of me hugging Chris! I could not believe it. I still sit in awe of that moment. It was an honor, and I am so happy that we had this opportunity to also meet Neal Casal, the lead guitarist, before he passed away.

It was weird, but interesting and fun things were starting to happen in my life that I had never thought would be possible. It was like the dreams I'd had as a child were being revived. I started to believe in the impossible and be open to all possibilities. Then, one Sunday in August, one of our worship leaders came up to me. At the time, I did not know her very well. She said, "I had a vision of you having large ears like Dumbo." I thought, *Where is this going?* She continued, "It's not what it seems. What I mean is, you have ears to hear God, and you do not need confirmation from others on what you hear from Him." Honestly, at the time I had asked God, "How do I know when you are telling me something versus my own thinking? When do I need confirmation?" So, as wild as it seemed, her words were an answered prayer. Two weeks later, I was in church, and I introduced myself to one of the elders in the church who was well respected for spiritual wisdom. His first words to me were, "Did you have a grandmother with a strong presence in your life?" The tears came like a flood, and I thought, *how could he know that? I just met this man.* Perplexed, I answered, "Yes." He said, "You have the strong anointing on your life like she had." I was still skeptical, but I was trying my best to be open to there being more out there than what we limit ourselves to in the human mind (Whew! The ego does not like that).

September was WAY overstimulating, but probably my most memorable month on record. On September 3, 2018, I dreamed I was talking to my Papa about how people hurt each other and that is just the way it is. I was revealing my inner thoughts to him. As I was talking to him, he was filling up a bowl with fruits and vegetables until it was overflowing. I said, "You know how people are." He said, "No, not all people are like what you are thinking. Sometimes, there are people who are like that, but then sometimes there are people that will give you more, give in abundance, like this bowl." I was dreaming in what I thought to be metaphors, and when I awoke, I immediately knew the meaning of the metaphor: "God is going to abundantly bless our relationships with people in the future as represented by the overflowing fruits and vegetables in the bowl." The dream felt so real, since my Papa was someone I knew and trusted to give advice. He represented wisdom from God, and I could not help but believe it.

I remember it was September 4, 2018, my sister's birthday, and everything I had read that day was a recurring message that God can do the impossible and that he would put me where I needed to be when I needed to be there. I was not sure what it meant at the time, but I held onto it in my memory bank. I had never had so many back-to-back messages in visions, in dreams, and from people. It had me curious, and I was caught up in a new venture of asking God to help me to know Him better. I was wanting to deepen my knowledge and wisdom, but more importantly to me was wanting to know more of His love. I wanted to feel more of what He felt in his heart.

A few days later, I attended a prophecy class, thinking maybe someone could help me with these experiences I was having with dreams, visions, and weird intuitive feelings about things happening in the present and the future. I had made my mind up that if people got too weird and spooky, I was leaving. I showed up, and the same lady that spoke at the conference I had attended where I had dreamed about the escalator was there. I thought maybe I was supposed to be there. I looked up and saw the Scripture Joshua 1:9 posted on the wall. I think my jaw dropped to the floor. I thought back to the card my Mema had given to me as a child. My mind was blown, or so I thought, until the real mind-blowing moments came. The lady from the conference, the class teacher, and other classmates all went on to give me the following prophetic words: "You have a sense of humor. You are God's joy. God sees you. God has not abandoned you. He has been with you all along. All the hurt and darkness of your past will serve a purpose to help others. You are a light, a beacon of hope for others, and you do not even know how much. You are a representation of Jesus and His spirit. You are gentle with a heart full of love. You are gentle, yet you are fierce and ready to go to battle when someone's hope is attacked. You are stronger than you think. What God reveals to you in the spiritual realm, not everyone is cut out for. You see what others do not see. You are made to stand up for those who cannot stand up for themselves. You are a strong force to be reckoned with. God sees your childlike love and faith and loves it. He sees all the hurt you have endured and how you have handled it, still giving thanks and being joyful. He is going to reward you. Nothing of your past is not redemptive. Everything is used for His purpose. You are a sweet, pure, and loving spirit, yet so strong." All I could do was cry in awe of that moment. These people knew nothing about me, so I knew this was a message from God, and he was using these people as a vehicle to deliver the message. What I heard in that moment was everything I that wanted, everything that I felt about who I thought I was called to be, everything my Mema had said about me. It also aligned with what my mentors had said about me. I finally understood in that moment that God was already using me and my hard life experiences to help others, only I never thought about all the people I had already helped that had lived through similar experiences as me. My purpose got clearer. I realized that I was called specifically to help provide people hope. I was already doing it, and there would be more people I would help heal in the future.

After these new discoveries of the prophetic and trying to learn a prayer language, I was skeptical and excited at the same time. Something felt aligned in my spirit, like I was getting it right. I was on the right path to knowing more about myself and God and His plan for my life.

Then it all got put to the test, but this is not what I had in mind. Will and I were at a theater to hear one of his favorite blues singers, Taj Mahal. We had just finished an amazing dinner. We walked to the theater. We were in the second row and so excited to see the many instruments that were already on stage. Five minutes before showtime, Will started leaning on me. I said, "Could you please stop messing around." I pushed him up, but he leaned back down, nuzzling my shoulder. "Will, stop messing around," I said, in a playful way. I crouched down to kiss him, but he did not look like himself. When he sat up, I asked, "Are you okay?" He said, slowly, "Y-e-s," but I knew something was not right." Suddenly, Will turned gray and could not breathe. I yelled for help. People crowded around. If you have ever been in an emergency, you will understand me when I say I had a thousand thoughts in those few moments. One that came to mind was when my sister's boyfriend had died, and I had said no, no more loss! I said, "Don't let him die God!" I felt frozen to the outside world with a screaming panic on the inside. I could not breathe, and time stopped.

I watched as all these people crowded around, which now included nurses and doctors, yet nothing was changing with Will. He was still incoherent, sweating, had no color, and was unable to breathe. Then, all of a sudden, I felt like I was snatched up out of panic mode. I put my hands on Will and started praying in my prayer language, very loudly, like this fierce mighty lion I did not recognize. While I know this appeared to be crazy, none of that mattered in the moment. As I was praying, we all watched Will start breathing again. People did not know what to think, but they were not judging because it was working. I could not believe it, and it seems so crazy writing it and reflecting on it. When Will became coherent he said, "I felt like something was on top of me." I said in a joking manner (with my inappropriately timed humor), "Oh, that was just your crazy wife praying in this crazy thing called a prayer language with the Holy Spirit as my sidekick. I get it, God, I believe now." As I looked up, I said, "Sorry you always have to show me things the hard way."

I really believed the stress of the lawsuit led to this happening to Will. It turns out that they think he possibly had mini strokes and damage to one of his cranial nerves. He was in the hospital for five days, recovering. Again, even though the lawsuit might have led to this traumatic experience, the silver lining is that Will became more business savvy from the lawsuit, and I understood the power of prayer and of having a prayer language. I also think it was not a coincidence that my husband had once helped me recover from trying to take my life, and now I was returning the favor by helping save his life. While both were traumatic life experiences, the lessons we learned prepared us with gifts and skills that we have used to further help other people. I would have never believed the power of the prayer language until it just came forth from the experience of trying to bring Will back to life. I think it happened because I did not have time to overthink it. Also, I think it came from a belief that has been deeply-rooted in my spirit since He saved me when I was 24: that God always shows up for me right on time. As I look back on those early, dark days, He really was watching over and protecting me all along, I just couldn't see it then. Having God in my life never slowed down the challenges because we need to face tests to build character. The challenges just became more bearable with God, through the Holy Spirit, by my side.

On September 21, 2018, we attended a special church service. I had invited my sister. I was still trying to help her work through losing her boyfriend. She said flatly, "I probably won't come." She was still struggling, and I had noticed in our last interaction that she was full of anxiety and depression. I had never seen her like that. I thought it would be good for her to come because it would be the first anniversary of the death of her boyfriend. I thought maybe she could establish a new beginning after nearly grieving herself to death that past year. I started praying, and I asked other people to start praying for her to show up. It worked. She showed up, even though she sat there with her arms crossed, clearly showing me her hopelessness, whether she realized it or not. When the worship music started, I looked over at Will and said, "That tune is one of our songs you wrote in our ninth year anniversary book, remember?" It was, "Is This Love" by my favorite artist, only they are singing "This is Love" to show God's love. Then, suddenly, one of the worship leaders said, "I don't know why I started playing this and singing it, but this is for someone out there." The other worship leader looked at him because it was not in their plan. Through all the weirdness with the dreams and words I received about how much God really did love me and Will, I knew that God truly cared about us and all our family. I soaked in His affections, and my heart just felt warm, like it was growing bigger than my body.

The demonstration of love did not end there. The elder who was preaching, who had also given me the word about carrying on the mantle from my grandmother, called me and Will to the front of the church. I was freaking out in my mind because I did not like standing in front of large crowds. To have to do so unexpectedly was not my thing. He went on to say to me, "You have a strong anointing on your life. You are strong and fierce, but you need to see that is your true self. That is who you are. Use your authority God gave you. You will speak the prophesies He gives you and make declarations that will come to pass. You have the mind of Christ." Then he went on to say to Will, "You will build great architectures, but stop trying to figure it out and just believe." He said to us together, "You have a strong anointing together that is special, different than your individual anointings. Your lives will take off like a rocket, and you'd better hold on for the ride. It might be bumpy, but God is always with you." He held out his hand and blew across his palm to indicate the Holy Spirit. I could hardly stand, I literally fell to the ground. Before this happened, I believed that when I saw something like this on TV, it was fake or dramatized. I really thought that, until it happened to me. When Will and I came back to our seats, my sister asked me what had happened, just like I would have asked her, if I had not experienced it for myself. I asked my sister if she would be open to receive prayer from our pastor after the service. She reluctantly agreed.

Before the service ended, the elder that had called us to the front of the church had a box, and he indicated that he had forty-three pieces of Scripture to pass out to the congregation as prompted by God. This caught my sister's attention, as her boyfriend's football jersey number had been for-ty-three. The numbers also represented the number of letters in the words, Love You: there are four letters in LOVE and three letters in YOU. As the elder passed out the Scriptures, I was one of the people who received one. Mine was Ephesians 1:17, " ... that the God of our Lord Jesus Christ, the Father of glory, may give the Spirit of wisdom and revelation in the knowledge of him."

The service ended, and I walked with my sister to see the pastor. He started praying for her, asking for the spirit of hopelessness and depression to leave. I started praying and then I started switching to my prayer language (I was freaking out, but going with it, after all, it worked before with Will). My sister fell out. The skeptic of the skeptics fell out flat on the ground and was out for a good minute. I felt some-thing leave her while we were praying. As crazy as it sounds, we could not see it, but we could feel it. It was the first time I had experienced the battle of spiritual warfare (since Cuba) so tangibly. When my sister's eyes opened, she was shocked that she was on the floor. When she sat up, she said, "Ok, I am a believer now because it obviously happened to me." She said that it was the first time in a long time where she felt like a weight had been lifted from her. The next morning, she would call me and say that she had slept all the way through the night and felt rested for the first time since her boyfriend had passed away.

After my sister had recovered, our pastor asked if he

could pray for me. He said, "I pray the wisdom with your relationships and creativity comes to your art and writing. May God restore your childlike wonder and heal the deep hurts that you have been carrying for so long." He looked up and said, "You and your sister have been aligned in your thinking/knowingness before, haven't you?" We answered, "Yes." He said, "Those are not coincidences. God uses visions and dreams to speak to you." I remember getting goose bumps when the pastor said this, as my grandmother's wisdom kept showing up repeatedly in my life, even long after she was gone. We indicated that our grandmother had had these things happen to her, but we had never really connected it until long after she had passed. I am convinced that the prayers of my grandmother are still being answered today.

On November 18, 2018, after thinking about the surreal experience we'd had with Will almost dying at the music theater, Will decided to get baptized. I asked my sister to come. She said, "Don't get any ideas about me getting baptized. I will do it when I am ready." I said, "Ok." I asked some fellow church members to pray for my sister because although she was better, she was still struggling. That Sunday came. She was late for church. We went up to stand by Will to watch his baptism. God showed up again and had a different plan. We all ended up getting washed in the water. Both my sister and Will got baptized for the first time, and I got baptized again, so I could share in the experience. All the while, the worship leaders played yet another song that was significant to Will and I, "This is How I Fight My Battles."

How appropriate were the lyrics! As a bonus, we received the following words before being washed under the water to start anew:

"Will, God will provide you more clarity on the purpose for you and Natalie. He will also provide you wisdom and show you His glory. All the resources will be provided for what is needed. Stephanie, God sees you taking a step in faith. He is restoring a vision, and you will be back in alignment with your purpose. God will restore your faith in the father—your heavenly Father and your earthly father. All the things that brought about your abandonment issues will fall away. Natalie, you will have victory everywhere you go. Every territory where you step your foot will be yours. You are a blessing, and you will be a blessing. All the seen and unseen pain you have felt in yourself and felt for others in losses and addictions will be restored. You will start having victory after victory, and all the struggles you have had will be no more. It will be more effortless because God is going to take care of it. You have wisdom. You will have victories and territories in abundance, and you will have the favor of the Lord. You will come up out of this water with clarity on your purpose. The communication with you and your husband will improve, and you will start praying together like it is everyday conversation. You will grow stronger together."

The three of us getting baptized at the same time felt unreal. I remember shaking from the emotion of it because God showed up big time, once again. Watching them come up out that water, shake off the weight of the world, and start anew made my heart so happy. They had already been saved, but we would have the conversation about the difference between getting saved and getting baptized. Both are great experiences, they are just different. All I would ever say was, "Something happens when you come up out of that water." There is truth in the analogy of the water representing cleansing, and it actually feels like you are a new person.

Chapter 12
Soaring

On November of 2018, Sandy called. She said, "I need to see you. Can you come join the family for dinner? I need to talk to you about something important." I said, "Of course." We arrived at her son and daughter-in-law's house for dinner. I had this foreshadowing feeling when we greeted each other and each time our faces met. She finally pulled me over to the side and started to get emotional. She said, "When the time comes, can you please speak at my funeral? I feel like you understand me. Plus, I know that being a pastor, but not in the traditional sense, will be in your future." I said, "Sandy, even though I do not like speaking in front of large crowds, I will do it for you, but what do you mean about me being a pastor in my future? I am not a pastor, and I do not have plans to be one. Nothing against pastors, but I am not equipped for that role." She smiled and said, "You will be. It's part of your future, but not in the way you would expect." I thought she was confused.

As I am writing this book, I wonder if she meant this or if there is something more to do with this in my future that I do not yet know. Either way, I can see now that she knew something. I am, after all, writing this book in hopes of helping people around the world to have hope, and to believe that they have a purpose and that everything bad works for a greater good. I also remember the certainty I saw in her eyes. There is a certain look or certain conversations you have with someone before they pass. It is as if they know things prior to leaving this earth, and they become messengers, providing pieces of information that either in that moment, or in the future, become important for our life's purpose. We ate dinner as a family, and afterwards she said she wanted us to pray together. She said she thought she got her prayer language at a meeting she attended with a friend, and she remembered what happened with Will and me praying in my prayer language. We prayed together, and then the presence of the Holy Spirit strengthened in the room and our praying in the spirit became extraordinarily strong. We held hands, cried together, and laughed together. I remember feeling a warmth in my heart in that moment that I had not felt since my Mema and I held each other on her front porch swing during summer sunsets.

On November 22, 2018, I had several visions while in church. I saw the church expanding, my sister with someone and very happy, victory for Will and his partner in the lawsuit, Will becoming more business savvy, my Mama being saved and socializing with others, a dear friend I have prayed for for a long time being revived back to life, an aunt and uncle's relationship being restored, my Daddy reconnecting to his faith, me using my authority to help and love others, and people seeing the love of Christ through me. Some of these things have already come to pass, and I believe the others will come to pass as well.

On December 6, 2018, I was having another immune system flair-up with whole body inflammation, which causes my back to go out. I was in pain. Not being able to get around just does not fit my personality. Will had joined a men's group, and they wanted to practice praying for people out loud and giving prophetic words. I thought, *Why not? I will go and be a test subject.* I needed prayer because I was not feeling my best, anyway. The group gathered around and started taking turns praying and giving prophetic words. Here are the words that I received which were all relevant to visions or words I had previously received: "You are walking in the river of life, weightless and swimming in the love and the light." This was the exact vision I had at that February, 2017 retreat. I took it to mean that I was going to begin walking more closely with God. I also understood it be about how much He loved me. Then there came the recurring themes: "You are the giver of hope to others. You will be an exchanger for others, meaning you will give hope with one hand and help people lay down their burdens with your other hand. This is how God uses you. You are a beacon of light. You are a representation of Jesus' love. You do not have to keep carrying the weight of your family and friend's problems. God is going to take that weight off and lay it down. Don't worry, He has got it. God restored your heart, He can also do it for your organs. All generational curses will be broken. Like Ezekiel, you will call dry bones to life. You will declare things, and they will be, even the craziest things people do not think are possible. You have wisdom and revelation. Your grandmother prayed for you to carry the mantle. You were meant to free people. You are meant to help heal the sick. You grew up fast, but now it is time to relax, dream, and be a child again. God will transcend your idea of space and time and heal all your hurts. Jesus saves, and you will be His vessel and let others see Him through you; that alone will bring transformation."

On December 8, 2018, I went to a women's breakfast at church. I hesitated, as I have never really loved planned routine events. I went because our women's minister had similar struggles as me, so I wanted to show support. I felt like I could identify with her. As I was trying to socialize and get to know people, I asked a lady if she knew the woman whose husband had called Will and me to the front of the church and given us prophetic words. She pointed her out to me, so I went to introduce myself. As soon as we were introduced, she got right down to business. She said, "You are a prophetic prayer intercessor, aren't you?" I answered, "I am not sure what that means, but yes, I pray." She said, "It means the Lord shows you things as a way to intercede and pray on people's behalf; you have to know when and when not to share, and you have to consider the timing. These things sometimes come to pass." I was startled and thought, *That is weird ... and it has a name ... and this happens to other people too?* I wanted to scream, "Thank God, help me!" but instead, I listened to her tell me the words she had for me. She said, "Your prayers cut like a machete through the jungles of evil to free other people. Not only are your prayers strong, but you will make declarations and they *will* be. The Holy Spirit will lead you, and you will have every nation and place where you step your foot. You are wise and far wiser than you even know, but this is how God uses you to tackle major spiritual warfare. You are fierce and you kick butt, only it is not often visible to the outside world; you do a lot of your praying behind closed doors on your own. It is how God uses you, for strategic wisdom. You have the wisdom and revelation from God. Look at Ephesians 1:17." I never made the connection until I was writing this book that her husband had given me that same Scripture out of those forty-three Scriptures he had randomly handed out earlier that month in the church service. She went on to say, "You hear from God. Listen to Him, not others. There will come a time in which the way seems right, coming from others, but if God says differently, listen to Him. You will declare mighty things, and they will be. You see things that others do not see, but this is part of the gifts of wisdom and revelation you have been given. You will be able to interpret tongues and your own prayer language at times. This will happen alone and in crowds."

That night, I went home and had a vivid dream. I dreamed that I was sitting at my Mema's table, and I had invited people I knew to come to the table. These are the people that I knew who had suffered from anxiety and depression. Basically, the message was that everyone was welcome to the table with Jesus. The invitation is not just for one person or a certain crowd. His promises are for all. The dream quickly then flashed to a friend who was at the table, and it showed that he later received relief from his troubles, and that his daughter was instrumental in helping that to happen.

In January of 2019, I received an email from my mentor that said, "Can you please pray for Ben? He used to work with us and be a part of the cycling team. He has an aggressive cancer and is having a tumor removed from his brain." The interesting thing was we had worked in the same company, but I did not know him when I received the email. I took this very seriously, because it was not often that my mentor sent me prayer requests. Once I started praying, something in my spirit said, "Go to the hospital." I coordinated with Ben's dearest friend, and we planned to meet at the hospital at the end of the week. The day arrived when I was supposed to go visit Ben in the hospital, and my friend, Sandy's daughter-in-law, called and said, "You and Will should come as soon as you can, it won't be long." Will and I were able to make it in enough time to speak to Sandy before she lost consciousness. We exchanged "I love yous" and long hugs. I held her hand as she drifted in and out of conscious. After some time had passed, we thought no more words would be exchanged. While everything was quiet in the room, I started praying and singing silently in my prayer language, switching back and forth, praying for complete peace. Sandy opened her eyes and said, "I never knew you were as strong as you are until right now. It's in your spirit." I will never forget her crying, but smiling, as she said it. I wanted to provide her with what she needed in that moment, but what ended up happening was she provided what I needed in that moment also. That is what the selfless love of God does. It is reciprocal and overflows your cup until it is spilling over. I believe that when we allow our pure spirit to operate, and it is not clouded by the ego and physical wants of the human mind, these beautiful moments can happen.

As I left the room, I felt a pressing, repeating message in my gut, "Go to the hospital and pray for Ben tonight as planned." Appallingly I said, "Are you serious God? Really, while Sandy is dying? Can I just go on another day?" I was so mad, but at that moment God spoke clearly, and I knew I had to go because it was not letting up. I got in my car and drove an hour back to the hospital where Ben was staying. The whole way to the hospital, I was angry and crying, pounding my fists on the steering wheel, saying "Why, why are you doing this? Two hard visits on the same day!" I kept hearing God say, "Trust me." I arrived at the hospital. Unexpectedly, there was a visitor in Ben's room. He introduced himself as Ben's brother. He had traveled from out of state to come visit. As soon as he introduced himself, he spoke very deeply and boldly in a voice that was assertive, but cordial. I started second guessing myself while I was waiting on Ben's friend to meet me from work. I thought, *They are from Africa. What if they believe differently from me? I do not want to offend anyone. Maybe I should just stand by his bed and be encouraging and not pray.* I heard God say, "I sent you here to pray for Ben. Trust me." Wow, talk about one of my most uncomfortable moments ever. Stumbling over my words, I said to Ben's brother, "Do you mind if I pray for Ben?" He said, "Not at all. In fact, we should pray together." At that moment, Ben's friend walked in. We talked for minute, and then his brother said, "Ok, let's all pray for Ben." In my mind, it could have been a text that read, "OMG" in bold letters on repeat, followed by, "How is this about to go down? I am not even sure we believe the same things." At this point, it was going to happen, and I realized I was just going to roll with it and do what God sent me to do. After all, if I offended anyone in this process, I would just apologize afterwards and hopefully they would be able to see the genuineness in my effort. We all gathered around Ben's bed in a circle and started praying. We each had our hands on Ben's arms and legs. All of a sudden, my heart raced a thousand miles an hour. After all that stress and worry about whether or not I would offend them with my prayer, it turns out we all ended our prayer with, "In Jesus' name, Amen."

When we were finished, I heard, "See? I told you to trust me." As we wrapped up, some nurses coming off shift came to visit Ben. As Ben's brother, friends, and the nurses, who were all from different parts of Africa, started to talk, I introduced myself, but then became quiet in the moment. I had studied foreign cultures and the difference between individualized cultures and group cultures, and I was taking it all in—how kind they were to one another, how they cared for one another, and how from their country, even if they were from different parts of Africa, their culture was still, "Take care of one another like family." For a moment, as a white female with blonde hair and a thick country accent, I felt out of place, but then God reminded me He had sent me there and that we were all one. I also remembered what I had learned with my mentor, who was multi-cultural: If I am genuine and my loving self, based on their joy and warmness, they will receive me. So I stepped in to engage. They did receive me. In that moment, I felt like a child caught in wonder. I thought, *I want to know you better. I like your joy. I want to know more about your culture. I want to go to your home country one day.*

I thought experiencing the heat while praying over Ben was the greatest supernatural occurrence of this time, but that was just the beginning of the work God was doing. As Ben's friend and I were leaving, he said, "I believe in God, Jesus, and the Holy Spirit, but I have never experienced anything like that before." I explained that the only experience I ever had that was close to that magnitude was when I prayed over Will after he had stopped breathing at a concert. While none of us really know the outcome of praying, our faith calls us to believe and have the faith of a mustard seed. We walked away believing together that Ben was healing and that he was going to wake up and walk.

Will and I packed our suitcases and returned to be with Sandy and her family. Sandy passed away within a couple days of our arrival. It was time to face the eulogy. How was I going to do this under so much emotion and with the dignity and honor she deserved as one of the most wonderful women role models in my life? What would I say to honor her memory to her family? Then, a dose of inspiration came. I got a call from Ben's friend, who said, "It's been three days since we prayed for Ben, and he is up walking and talking." When I heard the news, I smiled and looked up and said, "Really God, three days later? You're comical." I believe God has a sense of humor. Again, I heard him say, "See? I told you to trust Me." The news that Ben was walking uplifted me, so I refocused that energy into writing Sandy's eulogy. I received the motivation and clarity that I needed, along with strong prayers from strong prayer intercessors that I knew. I prayed and wrote, then I rewrote.

The time came to give the eulogy. I opened the bulletin, and I was the last to speak after "Sunshine on My Shoulders" played. It was so appropriate, as I loved this song, also. Sandy and I both loved the sunshine. The song choked me up so much that I was shaking. I stood at the podium, a wreck, trying to get it together. While I started out shaky, the love I felt for Sandy just made everything else melt away in the moment. I felt the presence of God, and I could see the Holy Spirit at work in the room. I let go of perfection and embraced just being genuine. Again, authenticity and genuineness prevailed, and I saw raw emotions move across the crowd. Afterwards, either with a hug, handshake, or shoulder tap, people said, "The words you spoke were so fitting for Sandy." In fact, someone asked me if I would speak at their funeral and asked for my phone number. That is not really what I was going for, but it made me chuckle to myself and realize, *Well, obviously that went better than I thought.*

Just when I limited God again, He surprised me once again. A week after the funeral, I was at work, and I heard someone call my name loudly, trying to catch up with me. He said, "Hey, I heard what happened when you, Ben's brother, and a friend prayed for Ben. Everyone is talking about it, and now he is up walking and talking." After the conversation ended, I walked on and smiled to myself. I said, "You're pretty funny, God, and yes, I understand that I need to stop limiting You. I also understand that what just happened was like what happened in the Bible. The witnesses to healing multiplied with the crowds. Alright, alright, You can still do wonders today like You did in Biblical times. I believe you."

I had longed for a restful spring after a long winter. On April 13, spring started with an exciting dream that was connected to a dream I'd had the previous February. I dreamed of a world map with dotted lines through specific countries, showing my footsteps following the dotted lines. I was walking with Jesus. I knew the dream meant something, but there were so many ways to analyze it, so I had asked

121

my pastor about it. He said, "I think it is an invitation to the impact you can make, but remember you have the option to accept or deny it." That was a lot to take in, and I could not see how that could happen, but I remained open to it. I do want to help people all over the world, but how? It made me start thinking about travel more.

My work sabbatical was coming up, so I decided to focus on that. I worked with a travel agency. I wanted to do things a little differently. I wanted to travel to England, Scotland, Ireland, and Wales, switching locations every two to four days, and I wanted to have the experience of traveling by train, plane, and car so as to have multiple adventures.

Prior to my sabbatical in May 2019, I was asked to speak at the church's women's breakfast. It would be only the second time (the first time after Cuba) that I shared personal, intimate testimonies of the work God had done in my life. When it was my time to speak, I could not. I held my head in shame, and the tears started rolling. My past crept back up on me. The women's ministry leader came up and held my hand and stood with me until I got myself together. I was shaky, but I did it. Once again, God showed up with His overwhelming love.

One of the artists of our church had donated a painting for raffle. At the end of the program, my number was drawn, and I went to pick up my painting from the artist. She told me the story of what had inspired the painting. It was the story of Joshua, from Joshua 1:9. I thought back to the card my grandmother gave me with Joshua 1:9 on it and how it kept showing up in my life. The tears streamed as I explained to the artist the significance that Scripture had in my life. She was wonderstruck with joy and told me, "So God had me painting this for you as part of His plan. That is so cool." I said, "Yes, I guess He did."

It was time for the trip of a lifetime! I was finally going to be able to see all the British Invasion band, PBS masterpiece, and travel documentary landmarks! When we arrived to pick up our rental car, I knew it was going to be an interesting trip when we both went to the wrong side of the car as I was videoing. We laughed so hard. As Will drove with excitement in London, I closed my eyes most of the time. Before we even got to our loft to unpack, we drove into a protest, got stuck on a pedestrian street, and then had to back out with a mob of people around us. When we finally made it to our loft, I texted the owner to let him know we were there. A friend responded and indicated that the owner had a family emergency, and he would not be able to meet us until a couple hours later. We had jet lag, and I was so ready to sleep! We decided to walk to Covent Gardens to have lunch. There, I discovered what it means to be so tired you could fall asleep without knowing it. While sipping coffee, I awoke in mid-air just before faceplanting in my plate of food. Will said, "NATALIE! Wake up, we will be in our room soon."

Our time in London was interesting. We were there during the middle of two protests, one supporting a government official and one against our president, who was actually visiting the same week we were (which we did not even know until we got there). I remember all the colorful signs and the crowds. There were more people rallied together than I had ever seen before, not to mention the giant, baby-shaped dolls made to look like our president flying and crashing on the pavement like bombs dropping. We started asking around where we could park and then studied our map. My idea of having the rental car had been for the countryside. I did not factor in the trouble we would have parking in the city. After numerous challenges of driving around the city streets over and over, we finally found a parking garage. A guy in a booth, asking us for cash only, pointed behind him and said, "You drive down there." We were so tired of driving and looking for a parking place that we decided to take the risk.

We pulled out from the gravel lot and turned to the left, and there was the tunnel to the parking deck. Honestly, my first thought was, "Oh, God help us." As we proceeded into the tunnel, it was dark for a long time before we eventually saw a flickering light. I looked at Will and said, "Is this really happening right now? This looks like the scene out of a thriller movie." It felt like we drove a mile in before we saw a faded light over parking spaces. I looked at Will and said, "There is no way I am walking back down that tunnel in the dark." He said, "Me neither. Start looking around for an exit." As we parked the car, I looked down further into the tunnel and saw someone leaning into a black van, vacuuming it out. I looked at Will and said, "You have got to be kidding me! We have got to get out of here." He reassured me, saying, "It's not what it seems." I said, "Maybe it's not, but I sure don't want to stick around to find out."

We sat there with the doors locked. Will said, "Get prepared. As soon as we unlock the doors we are going to walk quickly to find a closer exit." We got out, and as we were walking, Will asked, "What is that in your hand?" "It's the pen from my journal. We might need it for protection," I answered. He said, "What are you going to do with the pen?" I replied, matter-of-factly, "I saw it on TV. If you get attacked and have a pen, you can use it to puncture the windpipe." He looked at me and said in a loud whisper, "I feel like I don't know you right now!" I will say I have always been for peace, harmony, and mediation, because I am an empathetic person. Conflict is too disruptive to my spirit, and I don't like the way it makes me feel; however, based on life experiences, when it's comes down to fight or flight, I will fight, if it is over someone I love.

As we walked past some bicycles, we noticed a spiral staircase. Will asked, "Do you want to go first, or do you want me to go first?" It was hard to make that decision because we did not know what was happening behind us because it was so dark, yet we did not know where the spiral staircase led. I went first, and thankfully, the opening came up into the gravel lot where we purchased the parking pass.

Once we got out, I had this sudden realization, "Oh no, we have to go back and get our car when we leave London!

With the car parked, we finally had time to enjoy London. My favorite experiences were visiting famous British Invasion band landmarks and seeing the breathtaking view of the Cliffs of Dover. We learned from the locals while we were there that we were lucky because most days were not as clear and bright and sunny as that day at the Cliffs of Dover. I thanked God in a whisper. Then I said to Will, "Jesus makes the sun shine for me." I had started it as a joke with my friends years before, but the idea originated with my life verse, Joshua 1:9, and the story of how God made the sun stand still for Joshua. It's a story I tell myself in hard times when I want to feel God's love and warmth. The really mind-blowing thing was that it started to happen a lot. The days following the visit to the cliffs, I learned that the roads flooded. We had made it just in time to see God's wondrous creation.

We walked all the streets of London. Then it was time to go back and get the car. That night before we left, I prayed for our safety and protection. I was so concerned about going back that I had trouble falling asleep. When I woke up in the morning, I noticed that Will was not next to me. I got up and walked into the living space. Will was sitting on the couch. He said, "Are you ready to go?" I said, "No, not really, but I am with you, and I have prayed about it. I am ready to go get the car with you." He said, "Psssh, I already got the car. I figured my chances were better by myself, a guy with one blue eye and one brown eye, wearing a hoody, rather than going with my white-blonde wife bouncing around in colorful clothes and rainbow-colored beads." I paused for a moment to think about it and said, "Yeah, you may have a point—although I hate to admit it."

We began our drive to see the Roman Baths with stops along the way in the countryside. During our whole trip, nothing felt as close to home as our drive from London to Bath. There were miles of clustering trees and rolling grassy hills in more hues of green than I could process. Just before Bath, we stopped at the iconic Stonehenge. We opted to walk to the site instead of taking the bus. I remember the tiny purple flowers and butterflies along the way. When we arrived, I noticed the place was surrounded with sheep and there were two lambs that had just been born. Will said, "Hey, remember we are here to see an iconic landmark, you can see sheep at home." I was mildly distracted by the cuteness and sounds of those little lambs.

We walked around Stonehenge, taking pictures of this beautiful place. All of a sudden, I felt a heaviness and an overwhelming need to pray over the land. As I was praying silently to myself with Will walking by my side, I looked up through the crowd of visitors to see a lady who appeared to be angry. She was pointing at me with two fingers, squinting her eyes in rage, and saying something I could not understand. She was holding a beaded necklace in her hand and shaking it while she was speaking. Although I had never encountered anything like this before, I knew that somehow it was spiritual opposition. I was caught between knowing I had seen it and questioning what I was seeing. I asked Will, who is both a skeptic and a realist, and he said, "Yes, that is happening. What were you praying about over there?" I said, "I just prayed for healing of God's land and his people who live here. I felt a heaviness, so I asked God to lift it. That's all." As we walked to leave the grounds, the lady's eyes were still following me, and she was still repeating something with a body language that communicated only of anger and vengeance. When we got on the bus, God showed me my prayers for the land and how spiritual battles had long occurred over this place. He also showed me that just like I had a gift of sensing, intuition, and spiritual understanding, so did this lady.

For some reason, I began to feel sick once we arrived in Bath—so sick I thought I was going to have to find a doctor. I had all my wellness vitamins, but they were not working quickly. I had lost my voice. My throat was sore, and I had bad congestion and fatigue. We could not make our day trip to Wales, and I was disappointed. I later learned there was a violent crime in the area where we were supposed to be that day in Wales, which was actually an uncommon occurrence. I like to think that God was watching out for us.

Instead of Wales, we went to the famous Roman Bath Spa, as I was doing everything to restore my wellness for this once-in-a-lifetime trip. After swimming in the mineral pools connected to the original springs that were said to have health and wellness benefits, I was a believer. The next morning when I woke up, I was nearly completely well. We strolled the streets, enjoying the street musicians, and especially one who played a rendition of "Hallelujah" in the Roman Bath Square. We ended our last day walking by a waterfront, seeing the sun set over a beautiful cathedral. Bath ended up being my favorite place on our trip. It just felt like home, like I had been there before.

Our next memorable excursion was the butterfly museum in Stratford-Upon-Avon. There, I had a butterfly experience like I have never had before. As I enjoyed my time there, I was pleasantly surprised when my husband captured a slow motion moment of my joy as I interacted with a butterfly which happened to match the bright turquoise color of my coat. The really cool thing was that I was carrying a cork bag that I had bought from a beautiful kindred spirit in Covent Gardens. She had asked me to send pictures of me using my backpack as I traveled throughout England. That video, along with pictures in Bath, the Cliffs of Dover, and Windsor Castle ended up being featured on their company's social media. It was a nice surprise and an honor to promote the work of talented local artists supporting good causes for our world.

As we headed to Liverpool and enjoyed Mathew Street and the docks, we had another strange encounter.

Girl Behind the Smile

We were sitting in the bar of our hotel having lunch when a girl approached to order a coffee. She had a bag and started counting out some change. We were not sure when or if we should step in to help, so we waited. In my gut, something felt off. She started talking to us cordially, so we started engaging to get to know her. This was not an uncommon occurrence for me, as I found that wherever I go, at least once a week, if not more, I run into a stranger who is just in need of someone to listen. Something still felt alarming to my spirit, so I started praying inside of my head. As soon as that happened, the girl turned away from us, even though Will and I could still hear her, and it sounded like a different person talking. Because of our experience in Cuba, we recognized the battle of spiritual warfare. No one was around to witness it except us. The bartender and servers were huddled off to the side, talking, not paying attention. It was early afternoon, well after the typical lunch hour. I wanted to reach over and start praying for her. I started praying in the spirit first, in a low voice, and she got worse. I wanted to talk to her, but Will recommended that in this case, we should leave. Her spirit became more agitated, and you could visibly see the effect my prayer was having on her. Will was concerned for our safety, but part of me was disappointed that we left. In this particular situation, my gut was telling me to pray, but not to reach for her. I have learned to always pay attention to my gut. Sometimes, we just cannot help everyone. I still think about her and pray for her when she comes to mind. I feel like I failed in helping her, but I will never know, at least not in this lifetime.

Our next memorable stop was North York Moors. There, I realized I had not even scratched the surface of seeing all of God's wondrous sights. In driving through the hills to reach Whitby on the east coast of Yorkshire, you could see the road ahead for miles. Our next stop was another beautiful area of the country, which was the Lake District. We saw our most breathtaking sunset there in hues of orange, yellow, pink, amber, purple, and blue. There, I had the most peculiar and enjoyable encounter. I was heading through the breakfast line when I asked the server, "How are you doing?" He said in his distinct northern England accent, "Just terrible." I was not prepared for that answer, so I said, "I am really sorry to hear that. I hope your day gets better." Moments later, I was getting coffee, and I heard a voice behind me say, "I am sorry. I just miss my fiancé." I recognized the voice of the server and turned around. He continued, "I am supposed to get married soon, and my fiancé is from your country." Then he said, "Guess what? My mom named me after someone from your country who is a famous musician. When she was pregnant with me, she used to play his records and sing to me and rub her belly." This is not where I thought the conversation was going, but then again, I have heard all kinds of stories in my lifetime, and I always listen to others and try to be encouraging. He continued, "I will give you hint, he sounds like you and he's from where you are from." I sat there and started thinking, and before I could give an answer, he said, "ELVIS!" All I could do was laugh and smile. I was going to correct him and say I was from North Carolina, but why bother? He was excited, and I could see how he made the connection!

Scotland and Ireland were next on our list. I have never seen such beautiful country! Belfast touched my heart. On the taxicab ride from the airport to our hotel, we met this older man who had met Van Morrison, one of my favorite musicians! As we got to know each other, he shared something with us that I will always remember: "Dog spelled backwards is God, and my mom always said we should treat them with kindness because they are gifts from God." Wow, that really left an impression on me.

As we took a tour and learned about the wars and neighborhood divides, my heart ached, especially to see the peace wall and an area still covered in debris from wars. The people we encountered were so kind and strong, yet humble. I had another emotionally moving encounter. This time it was in our hotel lobby. As Will and I had ordered drinks and were waiting, God said, "Give this guy preparing your drinks your guardian angel bracelet." I said, "God, that is weird—why would I give him my bracelet? I admit I stereotyped and told God this guy did not look like the bracelet type. I looked over at Will and told him about it. He looked at me strangely, as he always does, but at this point in our marriage, after all he has witnessed, there was enough data for him to support me, no matter how crazy it sounded. It still does not keep him from holding his breath until the confirmation comes after I approach someone. I walked up to the guy and said, "I know this is very odd, but I think I am supposed to give you my guardian angel bracelet." He got choked up and grasped it with both hands to show appreciation. He explained to me that he had grown up during the wars and divided neighborhoods. He used to fight in the streets, but when his son was born he wanted better for his son, so he had stopped. He said he was going to give his son and wife-to-be the bracelet to keep. I later learned from a leadership member at work that the guardian angel symbol is a very important symbol, especially with that culture, and that I probably did not even realize the impact I had had on this guy just because of the symbolism of the guardian angel on the bracelet. He was right. I had no idea, but God knew what He was doing.

We ventured out on our train ride to Dublin. We ended up beside a group of girls in a bachelorette party. It was interesting, to say the least. We arrived in Dublin, and I could not believe the number of people. Mostly, I just felt so much unity amongst the most diverse population I had ever seen. I loved it. Our first trip was to the Temple Bar and the surrounding area where we saw U2 memorabilia and the hotel, recording studios, and the street where "The Sweetest Thing" was recorded. One of the restaurants we stopped in was really nostalgic, and we heard they had good food, too. As we were sitting there, Will leaned over and said, "That is Coolio." I said, "It can't be." He said, "Yes, it is!" I looked and was trying not to stare, but I could not help it. Coolio caught me staring at him and then smiled. I smiled back so big, and I know he knew my smile screamed, "I know who you are!" Will said we should just let them be. "It is different here than in the U.S. Celebrities are pretty much left alone and have more privacy. We should honor that."

We returned from our sabbatical a few weeks later and were scheduled to attend a Michael Franti concert with guest Jesse Wilson. I had heard from a friend that Michael Franti was going to be leading yoga at the farmers market hosted at a local co-op. Will and I ended up going. I had noticed after watching him on a few social media clips that Michael Franti seemed to be carrying the spirit of heaviness. I thought, *It must be hard for him to travel all the time with his wife and baby son at home.* I told God that since Michael Franti's music and lyrics had helped me get through some tough times when I was sick in bed, that if I had the opportunity to meet him, I would pray for him and his family. He arrived, and as always, he was being kind and interacting with everyone. People were crowded all around him. I waited, not wanting to push through. I leaned in for a big group photo, but as I stepped away, I watched and waited. I said, "God, if you want me to pray for him, I will, but I need you to help me." Will and I stood there. As soon as I said that prayer, he looked at me, smiled, and stepped over towards us. I told him his music had inspired me and helped get me motivated to get out of bed at a point when I was very sick. He clasped my hands to show gratitude. People were mobbing around. I said quickly, "I would like to pray for you and your family, is that okay?" He said, "Yes." I was already in tears as I started to pray for peace, protection, and love over his family. He was moved to tears and clenched my hands tighter. I expressed my thanks to him, then I stepped back so others could have their turn to interact. As I walked away, I was processing what had happened. I could barely breathe. I kept saying to Will, "That really happened. I was just given the privilege to bless Michael Franti and his family." Will said, "And guess what? I captured it all in pictures." When he showed me, I cried with joy that my husband had captured this moment in time.

Later that night, we attended the concert. As Jesse Wilson opened up for Michael Franti, she shared this moving story about her sister. I felt the emotion of it all, and I felt for her. Then all of a sudden in my spirit I felt prompted to pray for her. I second guessed myself and thought maybe I was just excited from meeting Michael Franti earlier in the day. The impulse wouldn't let up, so I said, "Ok God, if you want me to pray for Jesse and her sister, then when I walk to the concessions, if I see her, I will do it." We finished listening to a few more songs, and I started on my way to the concessions. I was looking, walking, and reminding God that if I saw her, I would pray for her. I got my drink, and as I walked back I thought, *I must have gotten excited and misread all this.* Before I could even finish that thought, someone cutting through the bushes and pine straw bumped into me. It was Jesse! I immediately said, "I was moved by the story and song about you and your sister. I have a sister, and we have battled through helping people with mental issues in our family. I can empathize with your struggles, and I would like to pray for you and your family, if that is okay." She said, "Yes, of course." I started praying over her right there, but people started to crowd around. She said, "Walk with me." As we were walking, we continued to talk for a moment, and then she had to go. She was kind enough to take a picture with me, so I could capture that special moment in time.

At the end of the night, I thought, *What a privilege to be able to pray over two musicians and their families.* I think it happened because my heart intention was sensing that they needed refueling. I realized that there are so many people taking from celebrities—whether intentionally or unintentionally—and it must be so draining. I just wanted God to use me as someone who could help refuel/restore their spirits through the power of prayer.

In the days ahead, I started getting promptings about August 8th (8/8). Other people in our church got the same thing. On August 8, 2019 at 12:11a.m., I was awakened by lightening so bright through my window that I sat up in bed. I am someone who can sleep through anything, so this was out of the norm. Then I heard God say, "Write this down." I scrambled to sit up and get my phone so I could type the notes. He said the following:

"You will lead people out of exile like Moses. Remember what your spiritual partner at work told you about Moses? That was Me speaking through her. This is My sign to you in thundering and lightening. I will make the sun stand still as I did for Joshua. Remember your grandmother gave you your life Scripture on a card when you were a child, Joshua 1:9? That was part of my plan. As that Scripture says, 'Be strong and courageous for I am with you wherever you go.' You will no longer be a slave like Joseph. Remember that your mentor at work told you that story during your struggles when you felt beaten down? That was Me speaking through him. Remember the ending to that story, you will rise up above. The mantle is being passed down from your grandmother. All family curses are broken with you. You will call dry bones to life just as your grandmother did. All weights and unhealthy attachments are broken. Remember what Will's small group said, that the weight of your family and the load you are carrying is being lifted. Spiritually, you will take the pain of others with one hand, and let go of it with the other. This is how you restore hope to My people and not hold on to it. You will build the infrastructure of what I call church, which is not always the same as the world sees it. Your vision, strategy, and organizational skills you have learned in the corporate world will be used to further expand My kingdom. This gets coupled with the desires of your heart, but My desires for you are even better. I see your heart. You have My heart and mind. I designed you that way, in My image, on purpose. Do not worry about how to have a worldly positive impact on humanity, just trust Me. All things are possible through Me. It is time to enter the next phase of your life. Step out in faith to Me."

I had felt the power of the Holy Spirit in love, peace, and strength in a magnitude that is indescribable, but I had never had an interaction with God this clear and direct. For the remainder of August, the dream I had of writing a book about my life would not leave me. I kept hearing, "Write the book. Trust Me. I will meet you where you are."

The end of August came, and my great-uncle, my Mema's brother, passed away. He was a great encourager to all of our family. He and my Mema were remarkably similar in how they liked to encourage others to do their best. Both of them were huge influences in helping me see the reciprocal joys of encouraging others. He and his wife and my cousins used to come visit us every summer, so I was blessed to be able to spend time with all of them through most of my childhood and teenage summers. We traveled to Virginia for the funeral services, and as I was talking to one of his daughters, she shared some of his last moments. She told me he spoke of dreaming about my Mema right before he passed. Uncle Hoke passed away on the last Monday in August just as my Mema did. Also, there was a song that Uncle Hoke was humming in his last moments, "Because He Lives." I got chills and told my cousin that is one of a few songs our Mema use to hum and sing to me and my sister while working. Their mom, our great-grandmother (whom we never knew) used to sing it to them as children. This is yet another occurrence in my life that proves there is an afterlife and that God speaks to us in mysterious ways to provide love and comfort.

Conclusion

The passing of Uncle Hoke and having the time away on sabbatical really made me rethink my purpose and my direction. These things, along with turning forty, brought a change in my life perspective. In going to work every day, was I doing what I loved, or was I doing it just for the money? I kept hearing, "Write the book. Trust Me. I will meet you where you are." This went on from August until the end of the year.

Right before my Christmas break, Ben called me at work to say he was coming home after staying with his brother in another state during his chemo recovery. He was moving in with the friend I had prayed with when Ben was in the hospital the year before. He said, "I wanted to let you know I am coming home, but not only that. I wanted to say thank you for everything you did to help me. If it were not for you, the running team, and others at work, I don't know what I would have done." He went on to say he still had the picture of the elephant I had painted him, and he was reading the angel book of inspiration I gave him. He said, "You know, I believe God sent you all as Earth's angels." All I could do was cry with joy. I told him we should talk again in a couple of weeks, around Christmas time.

At the end of 2019, when I was on Christmas break, I started helping Will more with his business. I also coordinated with Ben's friend to surprise Ben a couple days before Christmas to share the presents the folks from work had bought him. He was so happy. He smiled and said, "I can't wait for your book to be published. I want to celebrate with you and Will." He started on the angel conversation again and how he believed a few of us from work had been sent to help him in a great time of need, especially since most of his family lived out of state or in Africa. He was so joyful that day. As we hugged goodbye, he said, "I love you, even though I didn't really know you until I got sick." I said, "Ben, the feeling is mutual, and everything happens for a reason." Little did I know that would be the last time I would see Ben conscious. He went home that afternoon to take a nap, fell asleep, and never woke up. I went with his friend again to go pray over him in the hospital, but this time it was to say goodbye.

Something happened inside me as a result of my experience with Ben. I knew by the end of my holiday break that I had to plan an exit from work in order to write my book. The impulse just became so strong, I could not deny it. Even if I went back to work, I knew I had to take a year off and write my book, because I also had the prompting that my book needed to be published in 2020. It aligned with another vision I had of Spiritual Awakening 2020.

I gave my notice when I returned on the second of January, 2020. I planned my last day for February twenty-eighth, to allow enough time for training my replacement and completion of assignments. Little did I know that when the Coronavirus outbreak happened and some of the employees at my company got sick, I would already be by the beach writing this book. Some of the employees I knew said that the timing of my last day was divine intervention. Some of the people who had the virus were supposed to be at my going away party. If I had stayed, based on my weakened immune system, I would have been at high risk for contracting the virus. I remember changing my mind several times on the dates, but God knew.

March came with much rest and thinking about this book and how the book would continue. I am not going to lie, it was hard to relive and rewrite some of these stories, but if it changes one person's life for the better then it was all worth the effort, because every life matters.

As I sit here now in 2020, I realize that stepping away to write this book at this time was part of God's plan all along. I am glad I trusted God enough to step out of my comfort zone and designate the alone time I needed to write my story and provide a message of hope for people. I now have a whole new appreciation for one of my friends who said, "You were made on purpose for this specific point in time." I knew people needed a message of hope, but based on the happenings of 2020, I realize how important it was for me to get this book published in 2020. People need a re- minder that all the good and bad that happens in life works for a greater good, as Genesis 50:20 says. It is my desire to free those who are reading this for flight. I pray you get your beautiful butterfly wings. Everything happens for a reason. If you have not believed that before now, or if you have strug- gled believing it, I hope you can see this message woven throughout the good and bad times of my life.

It started with my grandmother and the card she gave me with the Joshua 1:9 Scripture and how it reappeared later in life on a wall in a church that showed me how to use my spiritual gifts. It also showed up in a piece of art I won which was inspired by Joshua 1:9. I have been able to use my suicide attempt and my experience with my previous toxic relationship to help others because I can relate to their state of mind and help them overcome their struggles. My deal- ings with family members and friends who have medical and mental illnesses have equipped me to know how to help others and their families in the right ways, whether through prayer, listening, offering advice, navigating the social ser- vices and healthcare systems, or helping with financial man- agement. The healing from God for my abortion allowed me to courageously speak on a controversial topic that brought healing to many who secretly suffered in silence, some of whom have confided in me. I learned the story of Joseph from my first mentor, which became the basis for writing this book. I also learned how to overcome my fear and love all people of all cultures from him. From my spiritual partner, I learned about the life of Moses and how the very thought that we think we are unequipped to do God's work is actually the very thing that makes us equipped. God calls the unqualified. His love really is unconditional, and His power really is that supernatural.

God has a plan. I encourage you to look back on your life and re-evaluate it from the beginning. I pray that you have spiritual eyes to see and spiritual ears to hear from God. Then use what you have to live to *really* live and help others find a way to live, too. That which was intended to harm you can be used to set other people free. Join me as we HEAL (Help Others, Express Gratitude, Aspire to Be Your Best Self, Love All Beings). Rise up and reconnect to who you were meant to be, and live your purpose! God, I pray right now for anyone reading this book that wants to be set free, that You will set them free and show up for them in a real way like You did for me. Reveal Your purpose for their life and guide them in the plan You have for them. Shower them with Your love and peace. Heal their wounds and repurpose any pain for a greater good.

I once was that girl behind the smile: hiding who I was, lost in pain, never getting out of the cocoon and becoming the butterfly my Mema always knew I was. It is only now that I can look back and see the different stages I went through, that I HAD to go through, in order to be transformed and to see God work all this out for the greater good in my life. I am sure those who saw that frozen smile never knew the hard times, the pain, and the loss I was going through. My story is a reminder that we don't always know what a person is dealing with behind the scenes. That brave face may hide a heart in need of love and acceptance, something that each one of us can give. As I write these last few lines, I feel God directing me to get this story out! He wants you to know He loves you and there is nothing He cannot redeem—nothing He cannot transform into something amazing! He turns a fuzzy, earthbound caterpillar into the most intricate, colorful, free-flying butterfly! I feel His joy just thinking about that. Always remember the parable of Jesus as The Good Shepherd. He left the ninety-nine sheep to go after the one. He did it for me, and He will do it for you.